IwC
1 00

ƒP

ALSO BY GARY HART

Right From the Start

The Double Man

America Can Win: The Case for Military Reform

The Strategies of Zeus

The New Democracy

Russia Shakes the World

The Good Fight

The Patriot

The
MINUTEMAN

Restoring an Army of the People

GARY HART

THE FREE PRESS

New York   London   Toronto   Sydney   Singapore

THE FREE PRESS
A Division of Simon & Schuster Inc.
1230 Avenue of the Americas
New York, NY 10020

Designed by Carla Bolte

Manufactured in the United States of America

10 9 8 7 6 5 4 3 2 1

Library of Congress Cataloging-in-Publication Data

Hart, Gary
    The minuteman : restoring an army of the people / Gary Hart.
        p.   cm.
    Includes bibliographical references and index.
    ISBN 0-684-83809-5
    1. United States—Militia.   2. United States—Armed Forces.
3. Military service, Voluntary—United States.   I. Title.
UA42.H37   1998
355.3'7'0973—dc21   98-12302
                                                      CIP

FOR

Robert Dole

John Glenn

Daniel Inouye

John Kerry

Robert Kerrey

John McCain

George McGovern

Warren Rudman

An enduring government by the people

must include an army of the people

among its institutions.

—John McAuley Palmer (1941)

Contents

Preface

This book is intended to help reawaken a debate as old as the American Republic itself. In his definitive *History of the United States Army,* Russell Weigley asserts that the history of the United States Army is also a history of two armies. Through geography, inheritance from England, and democratic ideology, our country has evolved a Regular Army of professional soldiers and a citizen army of various components variously known as militia, National Guards, Organized Reserves, and selectees. Even the most casual student of the history of the military in America—and one is hard-pressed to understand America without understanding its military—is soon struck by the constant tension represented by these two armies and the political dynamic this tension has produced. This tension existed nowhere more starkly than between "the American Caesar," General of the Army Douglas MacArthur and the humble Missouri National Guard captain, Harry S Truman, in the twentieth century. But it also existed between Hamiltonian Federalists and Jeffersonian Democrats in eighteenth-century revolutionary America. And even earlier, the roots of the tension between the two armies can be found in the dispute between the aristocratic "Court" and the republican "Country" in late seventeenth-century England.

Since the military plays a *sui generis* role in the history of virtually all republics, and in the American Republic especially, anyone seeking to comment seriously upon it must perforce render his or her credentials and qualifications. Mine are more political than professional. By strong choice, I served on the United States Senate Armed Services Committee for twelve years from 1975 to 1987. To me, it was the most interesting and, arguably, the most important of all congressional committees. I chaired the Subcommittee on Military Construction and served on the Strategic and Theater Nuclear Forces and Seapower and Force Projection subcommittees. Membership on the Armed Services Committee guarantees involvement in virtually all aspects of America's defense system.

I was also appointed one of several congressional observers at the Strategic Arms Limitation Talks (SALT) in the late 1970s and attended several negotiating sessions between the United States and the Soviet Union in Geneva. I took a particular interest in nuclear arms control issues, largely from a selfish point of view. I did not want my children and their generation exterminated.

Because of frustration with the mechanical role to which Congress had permitted itself to be reduced, I undertook to organize the Military Reform Caucus in the Congress in 1981–82. Its objective was to redirect the defense debate from one dedicated almost totally to procurement of this or that weapons system to one that focused first on people, second on strategy, tactics, and doctrine, and only third on weapons. At its peak, the Caucus attracted more than a hundred members from both political parties and both houses of Congress. It made important contributions here and there but finally failed to achieve its principal goal of requiring Congress to focus on the big defense picture. In furtherance of this cause, in 1985, I wrote a book, *America Can Win: The Case for Military Reform,* with an astute former senate staff member, William S. Lind.

Since the United States is, de facto, an island nation, I took a particular interest in naval matters. I had also inherited from my insular mother a peculiar fascination with ships, a fascination which persists today. This interest never quite communicated itself to my Colorado constituents. The closest Colorado ever came to the sea occurred during World War II when, I am told, portions of ships were constructed in Colorado for the war effort. According to this report, the hulls of the transport barges in question were made of concrete. I never knew whether to believe this story or not.

Having been stuck, not totally accurately, in the Washington pigeonhole labeled "liberal," it was considered novel that I should take this interest in the military. According to the conventional wisdom, "liberals" were supposed to be indifferent at best and hostile at worst to matters concerning national defense. They were, in a word, against the military. I find this peculiar even today. It seems elementary to me that patriotism is owned by no ideology.

It was, in fact, an outburst of patriotic zeal that led me to seek a reserve commission in the Navy while I was still in the Senate and relatively advanced in years. In a stunning reversal of national policy and blessed by the collapse of the Organization of Petroleum Exporting Countries (OPEC), our government completely abandoned any policy of energy independence, preferring instead a return to dependence on imported oil, conditioned only by a nonexistent "free market," rather than conservation and development of domestic resources. Given the increasing instability of the Middle East, this signaled to me that we were adopting a policy of fighting for other people's oil. This turned out to be the case ten years later in the Persian Gulf.

My son John was a couple of years away from draft age at the time. Anticipating his call-up to fight in an oil war in the Middle East, I made the more misguided than noble decision that I could not remain in the Senate with my son in combat. So I took the necessary steps to qualify for some kind of uniformed position in such eventuality. Although I did participate in several cruises on board naval ships at sea, I never became an active reservist.

That is as close as I ever came to military service. Passing through my draft years between the Korean and Vietnam wars, I sought and received student deferments. After three years in government service following law school, I took up private law practice in Denver in 1967, as the Vietnam War was becoming both militarily and politically hot. I sought and qualified for a Navy law commission in 1967, but this program was discontinued even as I waited for the commission.

Although it is convenient now to say so, I genuinely regret not having had active-duty service. The more I have thought about basic citizenship, civic duty, and patriotism over the years, the more I believe some form of national service, military or nonmilitary, is a good thing for a republic. Education, family, career (not to say classic libertarian principles) all militate against it. Still, the principle remains: service to the nation, in whatever capacity, is a noble thing. Had I found a way to balance these other goals with active-duty military service, I would have been a better citizen and a better senator. One way or another, I have spent an eventful lifetime thinking about America. The more I have thought about this country, . the more I have come to believe that America at arms cannot be understood separately from America itself.

The instinct toward service remains, and I hope it always will. A small way to satisfy that persistent instinct is to continue to try to participate in the public debate, and even to provoke it when it needs to be provoked. Thus this book. The national defense should be the preoccupation of every citizen. Those of us given special advantage should not sit by while the nation steers a course somewhere between dubiousness and folly, when it persists in perpetuating a military designed for one purpose into an age in which that purpose no longer exists.

I have come to share deeply the resentment of those in uniformed service who are frustrated by the politician's casual acceptance of their considerable sacrifices. As portions of the society, and too many in politics, were contemptuous of the military in the past, especially during the Vietnam era, so increasingly are some members of the military contemptuous of a political and social elite that takes for granted their hardship, views them as samurai or chess pieces in some great war game, or marginalizes their crucial role in society. A congressional vote for yet another pork-barrel weapon is not "supporting the military."

There will always be experts in and out of uniform, some more genuine than others, to whom deference on military matters is due. I always sensed a direct correlation between having been subjected to hostile fire and a sense of perspective in military matters. The most persuasive experts were always those who had experienced combat. From World War II combat veterans such as Robert Dole, Daniel Inouye, and George McGovern, to Korean veterans such as Warren Rudman, to Vietnam veterans such as John McCain, John Kerry, and Robert Kerrey, those most judicious with the lives of young Americans were those who have looked most directly into the cruel eyes of battle. Apart from genuine veterans, the so-called "experts" do not know everything. They may be long on expertise and short on common sense. They may know a lot about weapons technology, wiring diagrams, military theory, or organization and management, and know very little about how a democratic republic should go about defending itself. As the historian of classical warfare, Victor Hanson, has said of early Greece: "Battle became an obsessive image in the minds of those who saw very little of infantry combat."

I do not by any means consider myself a military expert. But this is not a book about the military so much as it is a book about citizenship, the proper workings and structure of the American Republic, and the role of the military in it. On this, every citizen is entitled—indeed obliged—to think if not speak. The central thesis here, that we should base our twenty-first-century defenses on an army of the people supported by a nucleus of full-time professionals, will be dismissed by many so-called "experts" as impractical, unwise, even dangerous. That is to be expected. Too many established interests have a stake in the status quo.

No single step would more challenge the status quo and lead to the restoration of an army of the people than a system of universal military training and national service. Given the natural idealism of young people, such a policy would be much more acceptable to them than it would to political ideologues and military careerists. And even the most modest system of national service would go far toward restoring classic republican principles and ideals of civic virtue. At the very least, it would test the bona fides of those most eager to have other people's sons and daughters fight for their definition of the national interest.

If this cause of military reform is adopted by only a few thoughtful iconoclasts, if the "history of the two armies" is brought back to life, the purpose of this book will be served—and the American Republic will be stronger for it.

Acknowledgments

In a polemical work such as *The Minuteman,* care must be taken in acknowledging those who have offered help that they not be held responsible for the author's arguments and conclusions. This is especially true for military experts, including retired general officers, who may agree with this book's premises but not the conclusions it reaches.

Among the distinguished retired officers who offered their experience, insights, and wisdom are: Major General Francis S. Greenlief, Army of the United States, Ret.; Lieutenant General Bernard Traynor, United States Marine Corps, Ret.; Lieutenant General Herbert Temple, Jr., Army of the United States, Ret., and Lieutenant General John B. Conaway, United States Air Force, Ret. Each of these gentlemen dedicated his productive life and much of his retirement to the cause of our nation's security. Each was generous enough with his time to help educate the author and to critique manuscript drafts.

Appreciation is due as well to William Lind, Steven Canby, Charles Spinney, and Bruce Gudmundsson, all of whom have been at the core of the military reform movement for the past two decades or more and each of whom offered crucial insights, especially concerning the current state of our post–Cold War national defenses.

Professor I. B. Holley, Jr., biographer of John McAuley Palmer and Duke University historian, provided the professional historian's precision in commenting on portions of early drafts. The author also benefited considerably from discussions with and from reviewing work in progress of the journalist William Greider, national editor of *Rolling Stone* magazine, who characteristically is ahead of his profession on the issue of the impending crisis in the U.S. military.

Most important, considerable gratitude is due Major General Edward J. Philbin, United States Air Force, Ret., executive director of the National Guard Association of the United States, and to Major Thomas M. Weaver, his colleague who is responsible for the library and archives of the National Guard, for their consistent cooperation and responsiveness. This book could not have been produced without their invaluable assistance. Indeed, the idea for *The Minuteman* originated in a conversation between the author and General Philbin many months ago.

Finally, I wish to express special thanks to the faculty and students at Pembroke College, Oxford, and particularly its Master, Doctor Robert Stevens, for their very cordial hospitality during the Michaelmas term, 1996, during which time early drafts of this book were produced, and to a unique law firm, Coudert Brothers, for its understanding in granting this brief sabbatical.

Adam Bellow, whose literacy and catholic knowledge

make him more a collaborator than an editor, deserves great credit for considerable improvement in this book's substance, structure, and style. Philippa Brophy deserves equal credit for finding Adam Bellow and a publisher, The Free Press, still committed to the dissemination of ideas and the promulgation of political dialogue.

This book itself is an acknowledgment of the incalculable debt generations of Americans owe to the men and women of the National Guard and reserves and the citizen-soldiers—the authentic minutemen and -women—without whom our liberties today would be diminished.

Chapter 1

A Conspiracy of Silence:
Why Doesn't Anyone Question
the Military Status Quo?

The ideological twentieth century was a century of slaughter. Twenty million people died in World War I, and 50 million were killed in World War II. Several hundred thousand of these were Japanese civilians dead through the instrumentality of nuclear weapons thereafter used only to deter combat between superpowers. But even these, the ultimate weapons, failed to deter North Korean aggression, or Communist nationalism in Vietnam, or fundamentalist nationalism in Afghanistan, or countless local and regional conflicts since. Military theorist Martin van Creveld has calculated that, of more than twenty such conflicts since the end of the Cold War, none has been between two nation-states. Even as war achieved maximum technological sophistication, it was devolving downward to tribal use of Stone Age clubs and machetes.[1]

The historian Barbara Tuchman defined folly on a national level as recognizing that a policy is flawed or outdated, knowing that there is a more plausible alternative, but persisting in pursuing the inferior, outdated policy nonetheless.[2] The United States spent over four decades and trillions of tax dollars structuring a military establishment designed to deter, or if necessary defeat, the Communist bloc led by the late Soviet Union. Since the end of the Cold War, however, neither political leadership nor military establishment has suggested the need to reorder, reform, or restructure our defense forces to cope with a dramatically changing world.

It is not as if evidence of change were not plentiful:

- Vietnam was the first warning that troops equipped and trained to fight the Soviet army in central Europe might not be prepared for guerrilla conflict waged by low-technology indigenous forces.
- A ragtag claque of Tontons Macoutes initially chased away a U.S. expeditionary force from the highly televised beaches of Haiti.
- U.S. forces were withdrawn from Mogadishu after being bloodied in a savage tribal brawl involving mostly teenagers.
- Even the more traditional war of the 1990s, in the Persian Gulf, proves the point of a changing world. Over six months were required to organize, train, and deploy coalition (largely American) forces, negotiate basing terms with the Saudi Arabians, transport the elaborate logistics and heavy equipment required of a modern army, and develop reasonably reliable intelligence on the region and the opponent. Wisely choosing maneuver over attrition warfare, the United States and its allies

achieved their initial objective of liberating Kuwait quickly and effectively but failed in the larger objective of destroying Iraq's Republican Guard and deposing Saddam Hussein.

- There have been recent calls for federal forces to be used to combat drug syndicates rampant in the nation's capital.
- National consensus to maintain U.S. peacekeeping forces in Bosnia is fragile.

These and other experiences should have brought military planners to consider other post–Cold War force structures. Not to have done so is folly. But this folly has its own logic. It is a perverse logic that should be called Eisenhower's Nightmare. In his valedictory, famous more in its breach than its observance, President Dwight Eisenhower warned, both as president and as general, against the creation of a "military-industrial complex" so politically and economically powerful as to take on a life of its own. This was not, as some would have it, an afterthought, the retirement sentiments of an aging statesman. "This world in arms is not spending money alone," Eisenhower said in his first months in the White House and within the first decade of the Cold War; "it is spending the sweat of its laborers, the genius of its scientists, the hopes of its children." Nevertheless, a military-industrial complex we would have, and it is still with us, representing massive corporations, powerful labor unions, economically dependent communities and states, and requiring candidates for public office to endorse procurement of major weapons systems and maintenance of military bases no longer needed and which, occasionally, the military may not even want.

The massive Cold War machine is composed of: contract-hungry politicians who prefer to serve their self-interest by lobbying for dubious weapons systems, such as the B-2 bomber or the Seawolf submarine, rather than serve a greater national good by totally restructuring military procurement; a calcified foreign policy and national security priesthood cloistered in Washington think tanks seeking to salvage remnants of Cold War theories to justify its existence; security analysts conditioned to convert every tribal rumble into a potential "major regional conflict"; military professionals more expert in budget manipulation than troop motivation and combat leadership; business and labor leaders more interested in a piece of the Pentagon pie than in a thorough shake-up of an outdated, corrupting system. This great machine grinds grimly, ineluctably onward, searching for villains, whether stone-throwing tribesmen or desert quacks, to justify its existence. Self-interest provides many reasons *not* to question the status quo—but there is one overwhelming reason—a changing world—to do so. Not to consider serious reform of the U.S. military to respond to this changing world is, by any definition, folly on a classic scale.

An army *of* the people is, ipso facto, an army supported *by* the people. Because it is not an army of the people, support for the current Cold War permanent standing Army in peacetime will last only so long as the American economy is expanding. Even a casual glance at recent economic history, however, shows this current expansion will not last forever. Booms give way to busts because the economic gods insist on market "corrections" and "adjustments." When the economic cycle turns downward, inevitably sooner rather than later and surely before the turn of the century, revenues to the federal Treasury will diminish, the military budget will look disproportionately large, and an anxious public will finally raise questions as to whether we actually need a Cold War military. Typically, politicians will be tempted to cut and slash in the short term rather than undertake the more complex task of reform in the long term. We will end up with a somewhat smaller Cold War army, demoralized, alienated from the people, and still no better prepared for the chaotic twenty-first-century world.

Our thesis is this: post–Cold War history has presented both the opportunity and the necessity of converting our current large, standing, Regular Army to a smaller, rapid-deployment, expeditionary-intervention force backed up in the event of longer-term deployments by a larger, better-trained, and better-equipped citizen reserve army.

The issue between large regular and small reserve armies on the one hand and smaller regular and larger reserve armies on the other is not one of military competence. The often-challenged Israeli military, for example, follows the second model. Indeed, it is not principally a military issue at all. It is a political issue in the classic sense and thus an issue of civic values. It is an issue of the kind of country we are and what kind of people we want ourselves to be. Arguably, the way a nation structures its defenses is the clearest way of defining itself and its values.

Re-creation of an army of the people should not be undertaken *principally* to save money. It should be less costly to maintain a reserve rather than a permanent standing force. And a persuasive case has yet to be made—aside from the generic argument that "the world is a dangerous place"—for spending $250 to $300 billion for a Cold War army to fight a defunct Soviet threat in the post–Cold War century. But the reform proposed here is not advocated primarily as a budgetary matter. Politically (with a capital P) this proposal is not presented as a leftist, antimilitary vendetta. It is, rather, a recognition of the central importance some form of defense must continue to play in guaranteeing future American national security that prompts this proposal for major military reform required in a new century of capricious challenges. Politically (with a small p), requiring political leadership to explain the national interest that requires a reserve call-up in a crisis or conflict is an important constraint on leadership's otherwise unilateral authority and is a vivid means of engaging citizens in decisions that affect their, and their sons' and daughters', lives.

Our current military establishment evolved in response to the realities of the twentieth century. These realities include: fascism's threat to conquer Europe; Communism's threat to impose its will by force on Western Europe; North Korea's invasion of South Korea; the Communist insurgency in Southeast Asia; China's emergence as a military power; concern for Japan's security; regional conflict in the Middle East; continued reliance by the United States and its allies on Persian Gulf oil; and, most recently, the rise of terrorism and radical fundamentalism.

Although certain of these realities will persist into the twenty-first century, fundamentally the Cold War realities that U.S. military forces were structured to defend against no longer exist.[3] The single most important new global reality is the unforeseen, uncelebrated end of the Cold War. The mystery behind the dearth of celebration may rest in part with some embarrassment felt by professional cold warriors who did not see the collapse of the Soviet system coming and who, indeed, believed it never would. It may also have reflected a sober and mature judgment by Western democracies to avoid a demonstration of triumphalism embarrassing to our former adversaries. But most likely, those with a powerful stake in the status quo wished to avoid the natural public desire for demobilization of military forces on the occasion of a great victory. "There are always troubles in the world" quickly became the new doctrine of national security "experts" and foreign policy elites, and few, if any, raised the critical question as to why the United States might be required to project a massive—and massively costly—permanent standing military and military-industrial complex, designed to prosecute a protracted war against the Soviet Union, into a new century in which the Soviet Union existed only for curious historians to pick and sort among its pathetic rubble. Besides, the permanent standing army, being both professional and very large for the first time in American history, there were no citizen conscripts demanding demobilization in order to return to an involuntarily interrupted civilian life.

And this is the point. A permanent standing military seeks causes for its continued existence and resources to maintain itself. A citizen army—an army of the people—participates in the debate as to why it exists, what threat it must repel, and how and where it might be used. For a democratic republic, there is a world of difference between these two institutions. This very difference, and the reasons for it, is the subject of this book. The post–Cold War era and the dawn of a new century provide the occasion for a public debate on this subject, a subject less about what might threaten us and more about who we are.

Indeed, our constitutional history requires this debate at this time. Few subjects preoccupied the Founders of the American Republic more than that of whether to maintain a standing army in time of peace. On this question, as in others, two strains of strongly held public opinion, bracketed by Alexander Hamilton on the one hand and Patrick Henry on the other, would be laid down for debate well into the nation's third century. "If we mean to be a commercial people, or even to be secure on our Atlantic side," said Hamilton, anticipating late-twentieth-century American foreign policy, "we must endeavor, as soon as possible, to have a navy. To this purpose there must be dockyards and arsenals [at home and abroad]; and for the defense of these, fortifications, and probably garrisons." Thus, Hamilton, the commercial Federalist, anticipated the Persian Gulf War by just over two centuries. "A standing army we shall have," thundered the anti-Federalist Henry in response, "to execute the execrable commands of tyranny." Echoes of this sentiment resonated in the rhetoric of Vietnam protest.

More is at stake in this debate now, as then, than simply the question of allocation of financial resources between civilian and military needs. This is not to say that public expenditures in excess of $250 billion annually in time of peace is inconsequential. But money is not the only or even the principal issue. At issue also is the greater latitude possessed by a commander-in-chief to commit a permanent standing army than to commit a militia-reserve army. At issue is the role and responsibility of the citizen in defense of the nation. At issue is the Founders' intention that state-maintained militias play a role in securing the nation, and thus the true reason for the constitutional guarantee of the right to bear arms. At issue is whether technology requires a military professionalism at odds with the republican ideal of the citizen soldier. At issue is whether military matters, including whether, when, where, and how to deploy American forces, have become too complex for the ordinary citizen in a democracy. At issue is the sinister sanction given by America's leaders in the Persian Gulf War to the conversion of U.S. military forces into a mercenary army— Saudi Arabia's Hessians—for the first time in American history. At issue is the continuing tendency by Washington elites to define our national "interests," requiring deployment of military forces for their protection, absent debate and consent by American citizens.[4] At issue is a new definition of national security and a clear definition of threats to it. At issue, quite simply, are the values of our society and the kind of country we want to be in the next century.

There is an imperative to the reintegration of military issues and the makeup of our armed forces back into the life of our society. A society defines itself and its values in many ways, not least through the way it structures its armed forces. To abandon the question of the disposition of the lives of our sons and daughters to the "professionals" is an abdication of moral responsibility in a mature democratic republic. We no longer possess the excuse, conveniently presented by the Cold War and the threat of Communism, that military issues are too complex, too technical, too abstract for the average citizen to comprehend. Even our elected representatives in Congress, as I know from immediate experience, find it too convenient to leave military matters to the "experts," to give their proxies to colleagues on congressional Armed Services committees on questions of manpower and weaponry, to succumb to the imperatives of the Pentagon, to confess ignorance on "threat assessments," to consider only the jobs created by new weapons systems and not their effectiveness or necessity, to play courtier to defense professionals, weapons contractors, and prominent national security virtuosos, to sacrifice their constitutional responsibilities out of fear, favor, or torpidity.

The great secret of the "defense debate" (which is not a genuine debate), however, is that on the great issue of the role of the military in a democratic republic there are no ultimate experts. On the foundational question of America's role in the world and the means, including military means, for pursuing it, every citizen is as expert as another. For the coin of the realm is common sense. The question, simply put, is this (and all important questions can be simply put): do you wish to be defended principally by careerists or by fellow citizens?[5]

At best, professionals are efficient, skillful, and effective. At worst, they can be mercenaries, samurai, or bureaucrats in uniform. At worst, citizen-soldiers can be inefficient, ineffective, and unskillful. At best, they can fight like tigers at Yorktown, Gettysburg, and Normandy. Or, to put it in another way, if our goal is to help guarantee oil supplies for Japan, other allies, and ourselves, we should probably send a permanent, standing army and navy. If our goal is to defend our country from any threat, there is no one better suited to that purpose than an angry citizen.

Few armies exist in the abstract. They should exist for a purpose or not exist at all. For, in Carl von Clausewitz's famous aphorism: "War is nothing but a continuation of politics with the admixture of other means."[6] If we wish to protect an empire of foreign oil, weak and vacillating allies, and other countries' disintegrating borders, we should continue to maintain a sizable (and expensive) permanent standing military. Because, as history and present experience prove, we will need it. If, however, we see our allies as strong and responsible enough to defend themselves, our own energy supplies as sufficient to maintain a reasonable standard of living, and ourselves as an island nation largely immune from invasion, then we can and should consider a national defense based upon a citizen military—an army of the people.[7]

In the simplest terms, our military forces must be sized and shaped according to the threats they are designed to meet. Unlike the struggle between democracy and Communism, today's threat is diverse. It is many things—famine, erupting population, gangs with nothing to lose, monomaniacal mullahs, urban decay, terrorists with nuclear satchels, disintegrating nations, clans who seek their own nations, mad-eyed nationalists, anarchists, avaricious arms dealers, bloody-minded drug czars, samurai, Mamelukes, mercenaries, and war lords. For four decades, our principal threat was conventional Soviet tank battalions pouring through the Fulda gap in central Europe. We may soon come to wish for the day of such a simple, direct, definable threat against which conventional armies and navies could be structured. This threat was quantifiable and thus could invite a quantifiable military response. None of the threats of the twenty-first century is quantifiable, predictable, or directed only at U.S. national security. Little wonder that the Defense Department, State Department, and White House of two successive administrations have chosen to maintain the military status quo.

A foreign policy must be supplied by our national political leaders. Since 1991, they have failed to do this. Perhaps a genuine debate about the kind of twenty-first-century military we need may also have the therapeutic value of forcing a debate on our undefined twenty-first-century foreign policy. Perhaps also, the mysterious absence of a genuine defense debate since 1991, through two presidential elections, is but a reflection of the absence of any clue among our political leaders as to what our foreign policy in the next century ought to be.

Clearly, the nature of the military is inextricably interwoven with the nature of society's goals, values, and purposes. The military is neither a separate creature from nor a professional adjunct to the nation as a whole. It has become too much so in post–Cold War America—remote, isolated, largely respected, but detached. From the earliest Greek inventors of republics, however, through the republic's Renaissance savior Niccoló Machiavelli, to serious students of democratic republics in the modern age, isolation of the military from society is unhealthy at best and dangerous at worst.

This is not a warning against a possible coup, takeover, junta, or autocracy. Late-twentieth-century America is much too sophisticated for that. It is merely a recognition of Eisenhower's nightmare: the permanent establishment of an economy so dependant on military procurement that massive expenditures for marginally effective or unnecessary weapons such as the Seawolf submarine and the B-2 bomber cannot be canceled for fear of economic tragedy and political retaliation; an economy so dependent on foreign (and cheap) oil that it is worth the multibillion-dollar deployment of a half-million armed service personnel, with their high technology weapons, to recover and secure it; an economy so dependent on imports from Asia that it will maintain bases and fleets to ensure against their interruption.

Restoration of a well-trained and properly equipped army of the people as the basis for our security would have this effect. It would once again engage taxpaying citizens in the defense debate. Demonstrating the good judgment and common sense in which Thomas Jefferson placed such confidence, these citizens would immediately raise one issue—and, of course, it would be the central issue: what would happen if we incorporated military costs into the cost of doing business? What if we amortized the costs of the Persian Gulf War into the costs of Persian Gulf oil?[8] What if we incorporated the costs of our fleets and bases in the Far East into the cost of products imported from the Far East? The answer is obvious. Suddenly, things start costing more. Suddenly, our lifestyle starts looking more expensive.

And, of course, this new economics still does not include the value of one investment—the value of the lives of our sons and daughters. *Only* 157 lives were lost in the Persian Gulf War (too many by "friendly fire"). Therefore, it was a "success" (except to the families of the 157). The Kuwait oligarchy is restored to power and "cheap" oil flows again. We feel good about ourselves. But there is no guarantee that the next Persian Gulf War will cost *only* 157 American lives. It could be 1,570, or 15,700, or 157,000. If so, we certainly should have a permanent standing military, for it will be much more efficient and effective at securing these foreign oil supplies, and, presumably, its personnel will be better compensated for sacrificing their lives.

A citizen army would engage the American people in foreign policy, both political and economic, in ways they have not been since more than 15 million of them suited up in World War II.[9] This would be a very healthy development for the Republic. Leaders, establishments, and elites, not accountable to and therefore detached from the people, begin to speak a special language and communicate only with themselves. Not familiar with the special language, and thus considering themselves incapable of engaging in the discussion, the people unwisely concede too much authority to their leaders (thus encouraging often ill-advised adventures) or they become alienated, angry, and mistrustful. The discipline of explaining foreign military, political, or economic policy to the people is therapeutic for leaders. Any policy that cannot be explained simply, directly, and cogently to ordinary people may well be flawed. No more vivid illustration of this argument exists in modern times than during the Vietnam War, when President Johnson decided against the mobilization of National Guard and reserve units fearing, rightly, that public opinion, in the form of a direct up-or-down congressional vote, would crystallize against American involvement.[10]

Trust between leaders and people has suffered badly in recent years in America. Much of this mistrust has to do with the way we fought the Cold War. The American people generally shared with their leaders the belief that Communism was virulent and hostile to democracy, especially seeking advantage in newly liberated colonies and the impoverished third world. Direct U.S. military action might receive public sanction where it had the chance of succeeding with reasonable speed, was in support of a popularly elected government willing to fight for itself, and was designed to help a country under assault from outside invasion. But, during the Korean War, when MacArthur's brilliant Inchon landing and less brilliant invasion of North Korea brought China into the war, American and South Korean forces were driven back, and combat stalemated, American public enthusiasm waned. After repeated escalations of American military deployments, the Tet offensive, repressions, coups, and the collapse of any semblance of democratic government in South Vietnam, American public opinion caused the retirement of the Johnson administration. The Pentagon Papers revealed massive deception—and distrust— of the American people by their leaders, a sure recipe for mistrust by the people of those who deceived them. Systematic support for undemocratic, often dictatorial, governments, the CIA-led overthrow of sometimes democratically elected governments, assassination plots against foreign leaders—all in the name of containment of Communism—have replaced healthy public skepticism with unhealthy cynicism.

The exigencies of containment of Communism now having disappeared (except for North Korea), arguments of secrecy and elitist expertise must no longer be used to prevent the American people, especially including young people, from being immediately and directly engaged in foreign and military policy decisions that affect their lives. The most effective way of reengaging Americans' interest in these issues is to place greater reliance on citizen-soldiers, an army of the people.

However structured, the principal duty of an army rests in the defense of the homeland. Therefore, the citizen-soldier

THE MINUTEMAN

must be trained both defensively, to repel any invader, and offensively, to support American intervention forces in actions outside the United States. Except for a small band of Americans who once saw the Russians coming across the water (and perhaps now wish to substitute the Chinese), most Americans see their borders and coasts as secure from attack. (The use of the National Guard in controlling urban violence, illegal immigration, drug interdiction, and disaster relief is a complex issue to be discussed at greater length further on.) This leaves the reserve forces, including the National Guard, with the principal duty of supporting, augmenting, or expanding the regular forces in prolonged operations overseas.

Since, by definition, reserve forces are not full-time professionals—in the sense that military duty is not their principal career—service in foreign operations for prolonged periods of time represents a considerable interruption of their ordinary personal and professional lives. Most reservists understand and fully accept the ethical imperative and professional commitment involved in their voluntary reserve status. Indeed, given the disruption in lives, families, and jobs represented by a call-up, members of reserve forces will follow U.S. foreign and military policy matters much more closely than they might as ordinary citizens with less immediately at stake.

With millions of reservists, their families, employers, and communities anticipating the impact of conflict in remote corners of the world, presidents, Cabinet members, and members of Congress will be called upon to explain much more cogently and persuasively why U.S. military engagement in a particular conflict or theater will fulfill national objectives. This will present a direct challenge to Washington foreign policy elites long

16

accustomed to assuming public acceptance of military deployments of the standing Army as part of the Great Power game little understood by rustic or insular citizens.

Military deployments in the post–Cold War years—most notably in Panama, Haiti, Somalia, and Bosnia—have been distinguished for their ad hoc-ery. Few national political leaders or civilian commanders have hazarded rules for deployment of military forces. But certain basic principles—or rules of commitment—can and should be established:

1. American military forces should be used primarily to protect clearly defined national security parameters.
2. Political and military objectives must be clearly established—tangible, obtainable political goals must be stated in concrete terms.
3. The American people must support the use of their military forces in any sustained operation and be fully cognizant of proposed levels of military commitment and potential costs—including human lives.
4. Forces should be committed only after exhaustion of diplomatic and political means of conflict resolution and after local forces have proved to be inadequate to resolve the conflict.
5. Strategies, tactics, and doctrines intended to achieve the objective(s) must be well understood and agreed upon.
6. There must be agreement on the command structure of any military deployment, and civilian commanders who make policy should not second-guess military commanders tasked with carrying it out.
7. The proposed military operation must pass the test of

simplicity—the operational plan must be achievable in its execution.[11]

Rules for commitment, deployment, and engagement such as these must, of course, fit into some greater foreign policy context. National leadership has the responsibility to provide this context. But, if there are those in Washington who have defined anew the United States's national interest in this turbulent post–Cold War world, and a foreign policy and rules of military engagement to support it, they seem not to have taken the trouble to share this new vision with the American people.

Or could it be that such definition, policy, and rules simply do not exist? Clearly the pieces are there. Our interests include: continued support for our traditional alliances in Europe; support for emerging democracies, especially in the former Eastern bloc; free and fair trade throughout the world; security of our borders; peaceful, diplomatic resolution of disputes; participation in international efforts to address global issues such as pollution, population, immigration, poverty, and disease; and so forth. So far, so good.

But then comes the messy part, the intractable real world that resists traditional diplomatic solutions. What is our policy toward disintegrating nation-states in Africa and Asia and especially on Europe's borders in regions such as the Balkans? How shall we deal with militant Islamic fundamentalism, or should we deal with it at all? Are we prepared to make wholesale military efforts to stop international drug traffic from Southeast Asia and Latin America? Are we prepared to watch the televised slaughter of innocents in future Rwandas and

Bosnias? How great is our stake in preventing civil war in Russia? Given our continued reliance on foreign oil, are we prepared to go to war against anyone who disrupts it? Will we adopt a policy of preemptive strikes against terrorists around the world? How do we prevent our allies from selling critical materials to nascent nuclear nations? Will we bomb a renegade nation we believe to be developing nuclear weapons?

These are just some of the real foreign policy issues of the twenty-first century—not the easy, vague, comfortable categories usually given out as our "national interests"—and virtually all these real-world questions suggest a military commitment of one kind or another.

But if we have yet to develop a policy or policies toward these troublesome issues, how can we know what the military component must be to pursue them? A distinguished retired general officer refused my request to help design a new military structure, centered on citizen soldiers, in preparation of this book: "I am unable to be of help about shaping and sizing such a force," he wrote, "because I have no capability to assess the threat. Force structure should be based on threat assessment (long term)." Well said. But the truth is, no one can assess the threat long-term or short-term, because, unlike the threat of Communism, the twenty-first-century threat is not *one thing*.

In retrospect, Communism was an integrative force. It provided a central organizing principle for the West following the slaying of the fascist dragon. Strong reason could be found for maintaining a large, permanent, standing military force, integrating it with the armies and navies of Western allies, and forming permanent military alliances such as NATO. Since the early 1990s and the disappearance of the Communist menace, however, virtually all the disruptive forces in the world are dispersed and dis-integrative. In the late 1940s, Churchill might give an "Iron Curtain" speech and George Kennan could later write his famous "Mr. X" article on containment of Communism. But in the 1990s, no national leader has given a speech or written an article with anything like their comprehensive vision.

No one can be said to be winning, or losing, the foreign policy debate—because there is no debate. In this age of confusion, the vacuum of the nonexistent debate is filled by the forces of the status quo. For the twenty-first-century enemy is hydra-headed chaos. Aside from opposition, what is the conservative, or liberal, position toward chaos? If twentieth-century anti-Communist institutions are ill designed to prevent chaos, what new institutions might? Which of the ideologies of left or right is best equipped to stand against rigid orthodoxy, vicious tribalism, or blind fundamentalism? Are we reverting to a struggle—potentially bloody and awful—between what remains of traditional eighteenth-century liberalism in the West and such primeval forces throughout the rest of the world? If so, it is little wonder that official Washington, still struggling to accept victory in the Cold War, has produced no vision of the future. The new realities refuse to submit themselves to traditional, and intellectually convenient, ideological categorization.

In the dim dawn of this century of pandemonium, the military alternative proposed here is a simple one: maintain a smaller professional force capable of dealing with local, short-term military crises—a "911 force"—and a much larger reserve force of citizen soldiers trained and equipped to support the professional force where U.S. national interests require a larger or longer presence. This alternative traces its American roots to George Washington, and further back, all the way to Athenian democracy and the early Roman Republic. The arguments for this historic reform are more philosophical, social, and political, and less economic, tactical, or technological. Virtually all theoreticians of republican government have discussed the dangers of maintaining a permanent standing army in time of peace and the importance of a national militia.

Socially, reserve military training and involvement can provide educational opportunities to many who might not otherwise have them and the socializing advantages of young and mature men and women interacting across class and racial boundaries. A system of brief universal military training and longer voluntary national service, both military and non-military, would provide the manpower base for the citizen army; but, more important, it would help reawaken a sense of citizen responsibility, civic engagement, and youth empowerment. More than any other measure, it would reestablish the necessary balance between rights and duties in a democratic society.[12]

The link between the privileges of citizenship and the duty to share in the common defense is as old as the idea of freedom and democracy. The idea that free men must be prepared to bear arms, to be known as *jus sequellae,* derives from the Greek city-state that "made it a condition of citizenship that all free men of property should purchase arms, train for war and do duty in time of danger." This was the origin of the militia idea.[13]

The ideal of citizen-soldiers collectively forming an army of the people is central to the notion of patriotism. From the Greek farmer-soldiers, to the Florentine *cittadini* practicing military *participazione* to secure the *vivere libero e populare,* to Jefferson's yeoman farmer and the Minutemen at Concord, to the National Guardsmen wading ashore at Normandy, the ideal of the citizen-at-arms, linked to neighbors and friends, fighting for his own freedom, his way of life, and his country is a pure one. It is not an ideal based on paranoia, vague conspiracies surrounding a "new world order," European bankers manipulating global markets, or fear, suspicion, and hatred of one's government. The purpose of an army of the people is to rescue ideas and ideals from those who distort them. But, even more, its purpose is to link the citizens of the United States more closely to the foreign policy of their country and to the decisions regarding deployment of U.S. military forces by giving them a greater and more immediate burden in sharing in the national defense. Such linkage entails a price in disrupted lives and careers and even loss of life, but its rewards are great—restoration of citizen involvement in the nation's life, abatement of alienation, revival of a sense of national community. The citizen-soldier, man or woman, will have a more immediate stake in national decisions.

The end of the Cold War and the close of an exhausting, bloody century of ideology have brought professional armies, the abandonment of national service in conscription form, and the survival of the pure militia principle on the national level in Switzerland virtually alone plus, notably, in isolated bands of discontented Americans who have appropriated the notion to defend themselves in a perceived coming age of anarchy or, at the extreme edge, for war against their own government.

A word must be said to distinguish the national militia concept from the nongovernment (and sometimes antigovernment) militias that have sprung up in the post–Cold War years. The difference—and it is fundamental—is that the former is the instrument of the state and the latter are not. The national militia is organized, armed, clothed, trained, and—most important—paid by the state. National militia members are soldiers (from the Latin *solidus,* meaning "coin"). Throughout history, soldiers have tended to obey the orders of those who paid them (or occasionally rebel when not paid). The militia concept of national defense proposed here would be nothing more than a significant extension and strengthening of the well-established system of the National Guard.

One of the reasons a small but growing number of Americans have separated themselves from the state, to the point of forming their own armed forces, is their perception that the state has separated itself from them or is increasingly unable to protect them. Private militias represent a breakdown of the state. This is as true for late-twentieth-century America as it was for Weimar Germany, or Lebanon, or Liberia. Leaving supremacists and extremists, neo-Nazis and neo-Maoists aside, some private militias exist to provide order when and where state authority disintegrates. In certain urban areas and sections of certain borders, it is not implausible to believe this may be happening. To believe this may continue may be alarmist, but it is not incredible. Officials of the government in Washington, D.C., recently proposed a National Guard call-up to protect life and property in the nation's capital. Many will not walk at night more than a few hundred yards from the U. S. Capitol. When the state cannot maintain order, other elements will seek to do so.

By turning policy, particularly foreign policy, into a game by and for an establishment elite, the American state has further separated itself from its citizens. Troops are dispatched to Lebanon or Somalia, Haiti or Bosnia, with little support or comprehension by average Americans. Acting in this way, a government draws a line between itself and its citizens and should not be surprised when citizens draw their own line between themselves and their government.

By pursuing its policies through the instrumentality of a large permanent military, our government further separates most citizens from defense of the national interest. While isolating extremists of every stripe, the national militia advocated here would reconnect ordinary citizens with both foreign and national defense policies. By so doing, it would reestablish the state and its government as an object of loyalty for many who now feel excluded.

Virtually all of "official Washington"—the foreign policy elites, most military traditionalists, political insiders and power brokers—will vigorously oppose a citizen army. The very notion will be casually dismissed as unworkable, out of touch with modern times, contrary to trends toward greater professionalism in allied armies—at best idealistic, at worst totally impractical. To be able to deploy a very large professional army is to possess great power, to some degree ultimate political power. Those with power seldom like to see it dispersed or diffused. One of the great political struggles of the 1970s and '80s had to do with the War Powers Act passed in the 1970s, which required congressional approval for all but the most immediate and urgent deployment of American military forces. This act was a direct result of President Johnson's use of the limited Tonkin Gulf Resolution as virtually unlimited authority to make war in Vietnam. Even with this act, President Reagan and his administration thumbed their noses at the law and the more explicit Boland amendment conditioning arms shipments (and other forms of military involvement) in Central American wars in the 1980s on notification and congressional ratification. A president driven by ideological imperative, power lust, or who knows what agenda, and possessing the commander-in-chief's baton and a great professional army under it, may be sorely tempted—especially in a single superpower world—to seek unilateral resolution of a messy dispute. The surest check on such power is direct citizen participation in those decisions. The surest way to guarantee citizen involvement is to place the ultimate military power in the hands of the people. The surest way to transfer this ultimate power is to re-create the traditional army of the people.

Chapter 2

The Transformation of War

Defending America in the twenty-first century will require both a clearer understanding of who the enemy is and the structuring of forces and doctrines best suited to destroy his will to fight. The greatest mistakes our national security elites could make would be to go in search of the wrong enemy and to continue to pursue a conventional conflict theory based upon firepower rather than brainpower, which is to say a theory that battlefield success is best achieved through destruction of the enemy's manpower and matériel.

In a recent book by Robert Kaplan, *The Ends of the Earth, A Journey to the Frontiers of Anarchy,* the author says that, of the eighty wars since 1945, only twenty-eight have taken the form of fighting between regular armies of two or more states. Forty-six were civil wars or guerrilla insurgencies. The fighting in the Balkans, in the Caucasus, and elsewhere suggested that this anarchic trend was proliferating. In 1993, forty-two countries were immersed in major conflicts and thirty-seven others experienced lesser forms of political violence: sixty-five of these seventy-nine countries were in the developing world.[1]

The timing of the restructuring of America's military forces could not be more appropriate. For the twenty-first century is going to look a lot less like the twentieth-century Great Power chess games and a lot more like the fourth- and fifth-century chaos of decaying empires. As Kaplan graphically states: "West Africa is becoming the symbol of worldwide demographic, environmental, and societal stress, in which criminal anarchy emerges as the real 'strategic' danger. . . . A premodern formlessness governs the [Sierra Leone] battlefield, evoking the wars in medieval Europe prior to the 1648 Peace of Westphalia, which ushered in the era of organized nation-states."[2] Kaplan singles out Sierra Leone because it "is a microcosm of what is occurring . . . throughout West Africa and much of the underdeveloped world: the withering away of central governments, the rise of tribal and regional domains, the unchecked spread of disease, and the growing pervasiveness of war."

Discerning Americans will find this picture eerily familiar. In the five or so years since the Cold War's anticlimactic close, we have fought one resource war, in the Persian Gulf, and intervened in Somalia, Haiti, and Bosnia—not to say East Los Angeles—to settle wars between and among clans, tribes, and gangs. The savagery of the fighting in these and other venues, such as Chechnya and Liberia, Kaplan points out, indicates something those in the "developed" world—those of us in the stretch limos or, as some have called it, the "Volvocracy"—may not have had the stomach to contemplate: "a large number of people on this planet, to whom the comfort and stability of a middle class life is utterly unknown, find war and a barracks existence a step up rather than a step down." Kaplan quotes

Thomas Homer-Dixon, head of the peace and conflict studies program at the University of Toronto: "Think of a stretch limo in the pot-holed streets of New York City, where homeless beggars live. Inside the limo are the air-conditioned postindustrial regions of North America, Europe, the Pacific Rim, parts of Latin America, and a few other spots, with their trade summitry and computer-information highways. Outside is the rest of mankind, going in a completely different direction." Kaplan also points out that Africans represent nearly 13 percent of humanity but contribute only 1.2 percent of the world's gross domestic product: "Thus, as Africa's population relative to the rest of the world has continued to soar, its contribution to world wealth has dropped by a third in the past decade."[3] But the problems of Africa are mirrored in other parts of the world as well.

Kaplan's thesis is supported by a revolutionary look at the future of conflict. In *The Transformation of War,* Martin van Creveld argues that war between nation-states, the standard for more than three hundred years, is giving way to low-intensity, largely urban conflict between tribes, clans, and gangs.[4] "We are entering an era, not of peaceful economic competition between trading blocs, but of warfare between ethnic and religious groups," he writes. "As war between states exits through one side of history's revolving door, low-intensity conflict among different organizations will enter through the other."[5] Van Creveld noted, in 1991, that none of the perhaps two dozen armed conflicts underway throughout the world at that time involved a state on both sides, and virtually all of those conflicts fit his definition of postmodern war.

If Kaplan and van Creveld are correct, then the theory behind current American military force structures is obsolete and, quite possibly, the United States is headed for a series of military embarrassments at best and serious and unnecessary loss of life at worst. For our current military doctrine traces its origins to Clausewitz, whose strategies assumed a monopoly on warfare by nation-states. Clausewitz hypothesized "trinitarian" warfare, that is, warfare committing the government, the people, and the army. All three were necessary to wage and win wars. The government was the state. The people were the nation. The army carried out the political will of the nation-state. Or more precisely, the government directs the army to carry out its will on behalf of the people.

Clausewitz has dominated military thought for almost two hundred years. He saw war as one of many social activities carried out by the state and could not envision war outside the context of the state that conducted it. "That organized violence should only be called 'war' if it were waged by the state, for the state, and against the state was a postulate that Clausewitz took almost for granted."[6] This, not the sophistication of his strategic theories of conflict, is the central point for Clausewitz. And it is this point—war as an instrument of the state—that may make the father of the theory of modern warfare increasingly irrelevant to the coming age. "The whole of late 20th century strategic thought rests on the idea that war is an instrument of policy; and indeed Clausewitz's main claim to fame comes from his being the first to base the theory of war on that proposition."[7]

What happens to the concept of trinitarian warfare when governments less and less make war against other governments (states), people (nations) are confused about who the enemy is, and the army is prepared for warfare against other national armies, not against tribes, clans, and gangs? Van Creveld says that if the present trends continue, then the kind of war that is based on the division between government, army, and people will be on its way out. Unless it can be quickly constrained, the rise of low-intensity conflict may end up destroying the state. Then, he says, over the long run the place of the state will be taken by war-making organizations of a different type. What types of organizations take over may differ in various parts of the world. In Africa, argues van Creveld, war-making entities literally are tribes, "or whatever is left of them under the corrosive influence of modern civilization." Ample evidence exists in Somalia, Rwanda, Liberia, Nigeria, and elsewhere. In Asia's "Golden Triangle" and Colombia's Medellín cartel, drug gangs tend to resemble late-medieval robber barons or sixteenth-century Japanese feudal organizations. In Western Europe and North America, van Creveld foresees groups similar to the religiously motivated, drug-supported Assassins who terrorized the Middle East from 1090 to 1272. Various mafias, drug syndicates, urban gangs, religious cults, fascist skinheads, ethnic clans and nationalist groups, and ultraright "patriot" groups fit this model.

All these new war-making organizations are challenging the legal monopoly on armed conflict held by nation-states since the Peace of Westphalia in 1648. Once this trust is busted, says van Creveld, existing distinctions between war and crime will break down much as is already the case in the early 1990s in places such as Lebanon, Sri Lanka, El Salvador, Peru, and Colombia. Often, crime will be disguised as war, whereas in other cases war itself will be treated as if waging it were crime.[8] The complexity of the distinction between war and crime has been even more profoundly revealed in Bosnia. What if the territory held by guerrilla armies and urban mafias—territory that is never shown on maps, such as public works, transportation terminals, financial centers—is more significant than the territory claimed by many recognized nations? asks Robert Kaplan.

In the multipolar, post–Cold War world, conflict between nation-states is declining and is being instead replaced by conflict between subnational groups motivated by either religious belief, ethnic grievance, greed, vengeance, perverted patriotism, or twisted nationalism. Collective national interests become more difficult to define and, therefore, more difficult to defend by conventional military means. Extensive low-intensity urban conflict will exacerbate the breakdown of existing distinctions between government, armed forces, and people. National sovereignties in places like Colombia, the former Yugoslavia, and Rwanda-Burundi, have already been undermined by organizations that refuse to recognize the state's monopoly over armed violence. Armies will be replaced by policelike private security forces on the one hand and with mafialike bands of ruffians on the other in venues such as Moscow and St. Petersburg, with the difference between them not always clear. National frontiers, which up to now have been the greatest obstacles to combating low-intensity conflict, become obliterated or meaningless as rival organizations chase each other across them. "As frontiers go, so will territorial states," says van Creveld.[9] In the aftermath of urban riots in Los Angeles in 1991, Korean-American merchants quietly formed their own militia or protective service, complete with uniformed and armed security personnel, which patrols their ethnic enclave in East Los Angeles in a fleet of official-looking, militarily equipped vehicles. To the casual observer, it looks very much like a Korean militia on U.S. soil. One wonders how many other ethnic groups in other American cities will create their own armed forces in the coming years.

Even those who do not necessarily share van Creveld's vision of twenty-first-century warfare agree that the nature of warfare itself is changing dramatically in the wake of the Cold War. Samuel Huntington, professor of political science at Harvard University, in a book entitled *The Clash of Civilizations and the Remaking of World Order*, argues that the future holds three kinds of war—transitional, communal, and "fault-line."[10]

Huntington's foundational thesis is that the transcentury, postideological world is reordering itself along lines of civilizational heritage: "In this new world, local politics is the politics of ethnicity; global politics is the politics of civilizations."[11] According to Huntington, conflict in the future will occur not between social or economic classes but between cultural entities. The conflicts carrying the greatest danger to global stability will be those *between* civilizations (so-called fault-line wars). Huntington's civilizations include: Western (North America, Europe, Australia, New Zealand, and others); Latin American; African (sub-Sahara); Islamic (the crescent including North Africa); Sinic (pan-China); Hindu (largely India); Orthodox (Russia, Greece, and much of the Balkans); Buddhist (Southeast Asia); and Japanese. Huntington believes that a world that defined itself largely by ideological or political belief in the twentieth century is rapidly giving way to a world defining itself by heritage, language, tradition, culture, religion and, therefore, civilization. His central thesis is that "culture and cultural identities, which at the broadest level are civilization identities, are shaping the patterns of cohesion, disintegration, and conflict in the post–Cold War world." More ominously, however, "For peoples seeking identity and reinventing ethnicity, enemies are essential, and the potentially most dangerous enmities occur across the fault lines between the world's major civilizations."[12]

There were two major transition wars—the Soviet war in Afghanistan in the 1980s and the Persian Gulf War in 1990–91—between the Cold War and the civilization-war eras. The Afghan War was largely seen in the United States and the West as the defeat of the totalitarian Soviet empire by "freedom-loving" indigenous people. Huntington observes that, instead, it was the first successful resistance to a foreign power not based on either nationalist or socialist principles but instead on Islamic principles, that it was waged as a jihad, or holy war, and that it gave a tremendous boost to Islamic self-confidence and power.[13] Similarly, in the Persian Gulf War, the United States rallied its allies on behalf of one Islamic state, Kuwait, against another, Iraq. As the conflict evolved, however, and was denounced by Islamic fundamentalist leaders as a Western imperialistic war for Middle East oil, the peoples in many Moslem countries united against the Western-led coalition even as their governments continued to support it. The two wars, Afghanistan and the Persian Gulf, formed a significant transition in global politics. Muslims everywhere saw the Afghan War as a civilization war and rallied against the Soviet Union. Muslims throughout the world saw the Iraqi-Kuwait conflict as a Muslim conflict, came to see Western intervention in the Persian Gulf as a war against them, and rallied against the Western military presence as yet another instance of Western imperialism.[14]

Although Huntington does not argue this, the Vietnam War, supposedly involving a conflict between democracy and Communism, was an early, transitional civilization war between a Western democratic state and an Asian culture. This outlook gives credence to those in the West who believed the government in South Vietnam was democratic in name only and that the North Vietnamese and Viet Cong were motivated as much by a kind of civilizational nationalism as by Communist ideology. Seen in this light, the Vietnam War becomes a precursor transitional war between the age of ideologies and the age of civilizations.

In Huntington's context, the attack by Iraq on Kuwait was a "communal" conflict between communities within a single civilization. Communal conflicts closely resemble van Creveld's definition of future war—low-intensity, largely urban violence between clans, tribes, and gangs. Wars involving religious communities, ethnic groups, tribes, and clans are often "rooted in the identities of people" and are, Huntington agrees, often vicious, violent, and lengthy. Communal conflicts tend to be particularistic—that is, they involve a specific grievance that does not necessarily spread to like-minded groups or larger cultural identities. They also can involve adversaries of different ethnic, racial, linguistic, or religious background.

Fault-line wars, being by definition military or quasi-military conflicts between representatives of different cultures, almost always are wars between religions and therefore civilizations. Due to this characteristic, fault-line wars are most susceptible to engagement of like-minded entities from the same civilization on behalf of one or both antagonists and therefore of escalation and protraction. "Fault-line conflicts are communal conflicts between states or groups from different civilizations," says Huntington. "Fault-line wars are conflicts that have become violent." Fault-line wars also tend to harden quickly on both sides into good-and-evil—"us" versus "them"—conflicts where subtleties and nuances are abandoned and where moderating influences on both sides give way to more radical elements.

This is particularly true where religious differences play a role. Tribal or clan wars between entities of the same religion prove more tractable and soluble than similar conflicts among tribes or clans of different religions. In the latter case, the tendency is for one or both to seek the support of fellow religionists and civilizational relatives. That support has been much more available now that Cold War constraints, the threat of superpower escalation, and the controlling hands of Washington and Moscow have all but disappeared.

The fault-line war, involving as it usually does subnational antagonists, becomes substantially more hazardous when intracivilizational national governments or states weigh in. This usually occurs at one remove, where the same-civilization supporting power provides money and/or guns. But this almost always brings in countervailing support from states and national governments on the other side. Each side in fault-line wars has an interest in emphasizing its identity within its civilization as well as vis-à-vis that of its adversary. The latter is a subtle (and sometimes not so subtle) form of dehumanization that lays the political groundwork for "ethnic cleansing" or genocide.

According to Huntington, in the post–Cold War world, "multiple communal conflicts have superseded the single superpower conflict."[15] In the civilization era, Huntington notes, "conflict does not flow from above, it bubbles up from below." Regarding the Bosnian conflict, he concludes that, as a war of three distinctive civilizations, its principal participants received substantial help from a number of states which, with the complex exception of the United States, adhered to civilizational lines.

Van Creveld and Huntington paint different but not disparate pictures of the prospects of early-twenty-first-century conflict. Both agree that tribal, clan, ethnic, and especially religious differences will provide the pool of grievance from which conflict will arise. Both describe this conflict as emerging from brushfires in the grassroots. Neither is especially optimistic about the role of the superpower as mediator. Both see larger states being drawn into these conflicts if nothing else than as arms suppliers. Both seem to agree that the more the Western powers intervene in local conflicts, the more pressure there is to eliminate intracivilizational differences on the other side. Neither seems to believe that the superiority of U.S. firepower constrains antagonists in a religious-quarrel or fault-line war. Both characterize future warfare as nasty, brutal, and prolonged.

If superior firepower, more sophisticated weapons, and greater numbers count for less, what role might the U.S. military be asked to play in the coming conflicts of the world? A dominant power waging unilateral war for local resources against dispersed indigenous forces in a distant country for an extended period of time is the least likely scenario. Sending

top-flight professional soldiers with complex military equipment to fight a continuing plethora of local, communal religious wars in a dozen disparate venues seems equally unlikely.
Participation in a multinational peacekeeping force for a reasonable time in a region where peace and stability are of interest to the family of nations is much more likely. Fighting two
simultaneous major regional conflicts may or may not be
likely; but even if it is, it can be managed with an army of
citizen-soldiers drawn from a population convinced that U.S.
engagement is required to make our nation secure and who
are willing to join with the armies of other like-minded (or self-
interested) nations.

One is hard-pressed not to conclude that the United
States continues to insist on arming itself for a disappearing
world and preparing for the least likely kind of warfare. It is in
the nature of almost all human institutions to seek to preserve
the patterns of thought and behavior that have come to characterize and define them over time. Quite often, when one era
gives way to another one, mentalities harden rather than
soften. The preservation instinct is, for many, substantially
more powerful than the inquisitive, creative, or imaginative instinct. This is especially true when the institutions in question—the Cold War military and security apparatus of the
United States—were molded in an age that focused on the
nation-state and gave it a monopoly on organized violence.

When the order underwritten by that monopoly begins to
fade with the modern age and is replaced with more primitive,
less structured—dare one say less "civilized"—conflict, the security institutions of nation-states find it hard to adapt. In a
time of confused transition, the innately conservative human

soul usually finds it convenient to do nothing. Militarily, this is where we are in the current period.

Our plight is even more confused by the fragmentation of the central organizing principle of U.S. foreign policy. Part of the breakdown of the three-hundred-year nation-state monopoly on armed conflict is traceable to the substitution, by modern foreign policy elites, of "interest" for principle and morality. This substitution has permitted nations to disregard concepts such as justice, the logic of history, moral principle, and the natural rights of humankind in directing national and international affairs. "Interest," especially national interest, is a shifting, amoral notion. What seems in our national interest today may be otherwise tomorrow. It is a concept without roots in reason or morality that justifies virtually any action, whether exploiting the sinking of the *Maine* in 1898, misconstruing events in the Gulf of Tonkin, or selling arms to Iran to finance illegal operations in Central America. Depending on the ideological biases of a president and his advisors and policy-makers, national interest becomes an excuse for virtually any action, however immoral, duplicitous, cynical, unjust, or undemocratic. The substitution of interest for principle, especially during the Cold War years, has done more to erode the democratic ideal as represented by the United States than any other single factor.

Further, foreign and military policy based upon national interest alone creates enormous uncertainty when an accustomed arrangement fragments. Thus, with the disappearance of the "evil empire," America today is confused and adrift with regard to its global "interest." For evidence, one has only to look to the American experiences in Somalia, Haiti, and

Bosnia. (And, despite the qualified military success in Iraq and Kuwait, Saddam Hussein still rules.)

A foreign policy based on "interest" works well in the relatively straightforward environment of a Cold War, bipolar world where all is focused on the containment of a single identifiable enemy. (By labeling that enemy an "evil empire" we were able to make interest seem like principle.) Upon the fragmentation of that world, however, our "interest" becomes difficult to define and even more difficult to pursue. Sizing and shaping a military structure for a single superpower foe is much simpler than shaping military forces designed to defeat elusive tribal clans and urban gangs operating in highly inhospitable local political and physical environments.

Our national security elites—the Pentagon, the National Security Council, congressional committees, Washington and New York think tanks—have ignored these unpleasant developments. Instead, they continue to focus on the so-called "two major regional conflict" (MRC) strategy, which assumes that we may well have to fight two conventional, nation-state wars simultaneously in different theaters, even though the experience of the past fifty years has been otherwise. (The last such involvement of the United States was in World War II.) They continue to build a large, permanent fighting force equipped with expensive, highly sophisticated high-technology weapons. As the history of warfare suggests, however, the perfect type of an old model is consistently defeated by the imperfect type of a new one in actual practice. Or, as van Creveld puts it, "modern armies are, by virtue of their very power, like mighty dinosaurs; and . . . they are equally doomed to extinction."[16]

According to Admiral William Crowe, Jr., former chairman of the Joint Chiefs of Staff and former ambassador to Great Britain, the United States has never managed to properly downsize its military forces following a war or major conflict. What we end up with is not a military structure designed to respond to threats and conflicts of the future, but simply a smaller version of the force structure designed for the last war. In 1990, the last full year of the Cold War, the Army had 28 percent, the Navy and Marine Corps 37 percent, and the Air Force 35 percent of Defense Department budget allocations. Seven years later, despite supposedly thorough force structure reviews by both the Bush (the Base Force Review in 1991) and the Clinton administrations (the Bottom-Up Review completed in 1993), each service's percentage of a somewhat reduced budget remains virtually the same. The Bottom-Up Review (BUR) concluded dubiously that the United States should maintain ten active-duty combat divisions prepared to fight two major regional conflicts simultaneously in two disparate parts of the world.

This defense "posture," as it is sometimes aptly called, deserves much more critical analysis than it received from a Congress now reluctant to question the orthodoxy of military elites sanctified by success in the Persian Gulf War. What are the prospects the United States would fight even one major regional conflict without support from our allies? Is a major regional war more or less likely than a series of low-intensity, largely urban conflicts involving tribal rather than national forces? How willing are the American people to accept substantial casualties in either a major regional conflict or a local brushfire war? Are ground forces necessarily the most important contribution the United States can make to conflict resolution? Do we have the capability to deploy our present and planned ten-combat-division Army quickly? Not surprisingly, the appropriate answers to these questions contradict our current strategy and force structure. For one thing, the current U.S. "go-it-alone" doctrine neglects history. We have never fought a major modern war, including in the Persian Gulf, without allied support. Our NATO allies alone can muster ten well-trained, mobile combat divisions, and these allies share most of our interests in Europe and elsewhere. NATO still seems important enough to us that we are willing to invite the long-term alienation of Russia in order to expand it. Additionally, a number of allied or friendly regional powers, not least South Korea, also have large, well-trained armies. At least some of these forces would be fighting with us in any major conflict we envision.

Conflict on the grand scale is swiftly being replaced by low-intensity, usually urban, conflict between tribes, clans, and gangs. Such has been the case in Bosnia, Chechnya, Somalia, Rwanda, Haiti, Sudan, Algeria, and, where gangs are concerned, virtually every major city in the world, including most of our own. These are conflicts whose instigators are not impressed by U.S. combat divisions or high-tech weapons. Indeed, in most of such cases a U.S. military presence on the ground can lead to more antagonism than do peacekeeping forces from smaller, less powerful nations.

As in Lebanon and Somalia, the American people have shown a willingness to support U.S. military intervention in a conflict zone as long as U.S. casualties are minimal. Happily, this thesis was not tested in the ninety-six-hour war against Iraq. But one can readily imagine public response had the

Gulf War dragged on with great loss of American lives. Short of a direct attack on our borders, it is difficult if not impossible to imagine a scenario wherein a U.S. president could unilaterally commit American ground forces to a sustained, high-casualty foreign military operation.

American Cold War policy was largely based upon a cultural contradiction. We convinced ourselves, based on solid evidence, that Soviet-based Communism threatened Western democracy. We allocated enormous national wealth, in the form of military manpower and weaponry, to its containment. Yet, despite this perceived threat to our security and survival, we never implemented a European-style, national, conscription-based reserve system in which virtually all able-bodied young men [and today possibly women] were required to participate. Custom and history were too powerful. The United States has survived several major wars with a local militia system based in large part on peacetime voluntary recruitment. Largely because of this, Americans have not developed a belief in a social contract that expresses itself in the form of compulsory peacetime military service. It is not that Americans oppose the principle of compulsory military service as an obligation of citizenship in time of actual danger. It is rather because the United States strategically is an island nation that we have been able to formulate a narrow and restrictive definition of what constitutes "actual danger."

As the twenty-first century dawns, what constitutes "actual danger" to the United States must be redefined. With the increased size and stability of most of our allies' military forces, U.S. air and sea support for allied ground forces becomes increasingly our most important contribution to collective security and combined operations. As noted, our NATO allies have ten highly trained rapid deployment divisions. Superior American air and naval power combined with these well-trained allied ground forces is the most effective combination to deal with simultaneous conflicts. Politicians feel constrained from making this obvious point lest they be accused of "failing to meet our global commitments"—whatever and wherever those are. Thus, American force structure is held hostage by a monolithic doctrine based upon vague, undefined global policing commitments whose premises cannot be questioned for fear of seeming less than resolute.

Finally, and perhaps most important, how usable are ten active-duty Army divisions in real life? Here one runs into the very real constraint called transport, or "lift." How do we get them from here to there? Despite expenditures in the tens of billions of dollars, strategic lift—namely, troop and cargo ships and planes—operates under finite limits. And despite such huge expenditures, lift remains underfunded because it is less politically visible and popular than the more dramatic—and more job-producing—high-tech combat fighters, ships, and missiles. But the brutal facts of limited lift capacity directly challenge our current active-duty force structures and warfighting plans. "There is no justification to maintain all ten divisions mobilized at peak readiness during peacetime since *limits in strategic lift allow no more than five divisions to be deployed within 90 days.*"[17] Best estimates are that seventy-five days are required to embark and deploy a five-division active-duty force overseas; at least fifteen additional days will be required to return transport ships to American ports for lifting reinforcements. Follow-on divisions could not be deployed for at least ninety more days, and this presumes that everything works perfectly. All this simply means that the Army needs no more than five active-duty combat divisions, because reserve divisions can mobilize, train, and move to American ports long before the availability of lift capability to transport them.[18]

Given the natural resistance to external demands for reform and reduction in size that is common to all institutions, the U.S. military follows a well-established pattern. First, the proposal for change is studied endlessly. Delay is reform's most effective enemy, especially if (as rarely happens) Congress is the instigating agency. Senior commanders know that Congress's attention is ephemeral and dissipates quickly under the pressure of newer concerns. Second, the longer the time permitted to study force reduction, the greater the chance to mobilize traditionalist elements in the weapons procurement community, the retired military, the press, and the public. Third, the services can accept reduction through attrition, knowing that sometime later they can claim their forces to be hollowed out, weak, and not combat ready. The resulting "scandal" surrounding lack of readiness and weak national defenses will cause a subsequent Congress to appropriate whatever funds are required to restore a "strong national defense," that is, essentially the same force that existed before downsizing began. Although this analysis may seem cynical, it has certain patterns in history, especially when a large standing military establishment takes on the kind of economic and political power feared by most of our nation's founders and republican theorists throughout history.

It is folly to presume that at all times and in all places war always bears the same face. War has its own history. It has evolved over time from set-piece pageantry to mass slaughter, from spear-bearing warriors with painted faces issuing terrifying screams in ritual dances to the cold technological hell of Hiroshima. When war became the province of the nation-state in the seventeenth century, it took on a certain form to which we have become so accustomed as to assume it is eternal. Tensions between nations arose over borders or commercial advantage or ill-treated ethnic minorities or, worst of all, over ideology or religion. When that tension reached a certain temperature, some planned or random event triggered skirmish, retaliation, confrontation, invasion, prolonged and bloody struggle, exhaustion or defeat, conquest or negotiation, and peace. Then the pattern would emerge again involving either the same combatants or a new set of partners.

Whatever "progress" there has been in the art of war in recent centuries is traceable to science and technology. The age of modernity has made killing more efficient, therefore more detached. Hand-to-hand combat, providing the vivid experience of watching one's enemy's eyes as he died, faded in the twentieth century. Technology provided the means to deliver death at greater distances, thus removing what might ironically be called the "human element" from war. Only the most serious moral philosophers know whether this is a good or a bad thing. As with most profound human questions, the matter can be argued both ways. Men and women sent into combat can carry out their grim duties, killing the enemy without actually experiencing the suffering and death attendant on those duties—in other words, "push-button war." However, this same detachment eliminates the sobering firsthand experience of death and killing that normally builds human support for noncombative conflict resolution. Which is better, to see it or not to see it?

The nuclear arms race contributed one significant element to twentieth-century military theory, namely the doctrine of deterrence. Although the modern version of this doctrine was based upon mutual assured destruction and the terror of holocaust, it had its effect. However, this doctrine did not achieve much progress along the lines of what one might call the nonviolent aspect of war. This is an oxymoron in appearance only. Many of the great military theorists from Sun Tzu to Machiavelli and beyond have understood that success in war is best measured by sustaining the fewest casualties in the course of breaking the enemy's *will*. Destroying the enemy's body may not always be the most effective way of destroying his will to fight.

Not only has strategic reality changed; tactical reality has changed as well. About the time that "strategy" in the Clausewitzian sense of the word emerged in the nineteenth century, so did large-scale, crew-operated weaponry of the sort that today encompasses virtually all American military firepower. In fact, van Creveld claims that from the nineteenth century on, the trend away from individual weapons and toward large, crew-operated ones has been one of the dominant themes of modern warfare. The problem, he says, is that most modern crew-operated weapons—including specifically the most powerful and sophisticated among them—are dinosaurs.[19] Thus, symmetrically, dinosaur armies are equipped with dinosaur weapons.

Part of the reason large, sophisticated, powerful crew-operated weapons designed for the superpower battlefield do not work today is that the battlefield has become the civilian street corner, the back alley, or the high-rise buildings reduced, in Grozny/Mogadishu/Sarajevo/Beirut, to urban rubble. When the United States sent military forces to Lebanon, it tried one air strike. It lost two planes—total cost, $60 million—to off-the-shelf ground-to-air missiles, and that was it—no more air strikes. Lebanon was also the place where we lost 244 Marines to a single attacker, a religious fanatic with a giant truck bomb. That should have been a wake-up call about the changing nature of warfare and weaponry. The same thing happened in 1996 in Riyadh, with one difference. The driver of the truck walked away before the explosion and is somewhere available for another mission.

The sophisticated, heavy-duty, crew-operated weapon is no more effective in a cluttered urban environment than a conventionally trained combat division. That is because the "enemy" does not wear a uniform, is not marching in rank, does not deploy in conventional formations, and in fact looks pretty much like everyone else. Intermingling with enemy forces, mixing with the civilian population, and extreme dispersion have now become the normal practice in low-intensity conflicts, claims van Creveld. Even so-called "hard targets," such as command, control, communications, and intelligence centers, are increasingly being constructed in the centers of urban population, thus defeating even the most sophisticated "smart" weapons. If the smartest cruise missile goes in the window of such a facility, it will probably also wipe out the school or hospital next door. But fewer and fewer of these facilities have windows since they are increasingly being built underground in the middle of population centers. (The Pentagon has yet to release a report on the overall accuracy of "smart weapons" in the Gulf War, promised some six years ago. Could it be these weapons were not as "smart" as we were told?)

Van Creveld's thesis concerning the transformation of war is based upon the experience of the last two decades, which strongly suggests that long-range, computerized, high-tech warfare so dear to the military-industrial complex is the *least likely* form of conflict in the foreseeable future. "Armed conflict will be waged by men on earth, not robots in space," he says, and will more closely resemble the struggles of primitive tribes than the large-scale conventional war conducted possibly for the last times in 1973 (the Arab-Israeli War), 1982 (the Falklands), and 1980–88 (the Iran-Iraq War). Set-piece battles are being replaced by belligerents intermingled with each other and the civilian population, thus making the normal concepts of Clausewitzian strategy irrelevant. War will not be waged by remote, neatly uniformed men in air-conditioned rooms sitting behind screens, manipulating sophisticated weapons, and pushing buttons. Troops will instead have more in common with policemen (or with pirates) than with defense analysts and will use less, not more, sophisticated weapons. War will not take place in open, agreed-upon fields where armies meet in organized combat but rather will take place in complex urban environments. "It will be a war of listening devices and of car-bombs, of men killing each other at close quarters, and of women using their purses to carry explosives and the drugs to pay for them. *It will be protracted, bloody, and horrible,*" van Creveld concludes.[20]

At the close of the twentieth century the United States, the planet's single superpower, the most mighty nation in the history of mankind, is a muscle-bound giant that is prepared to fight the least likely war and has not made the adjustment to an age of brutal new realities. Few prospects presently exist for the United States to deploy hundreds of thousands, not to say millions, of forces overseas in a protracted conflict. If one of those remote prospects should emerge, in a war over Middle East oil fields, for example, it will most likely do so under conditions that would give this country ample opportunity to mobilize very large numbers of well-trained, well-equipped citizen-soldiers. There are many prospects for United States participation in multinational peacemaking, peacekeeping, humanitarian relief, police actions. Given recent experience, the manpower levels for such operations will be in the range of 5,000 to 10,000 troops. Indeed, escape from the new realities of warfare will not be an option. Robert Kaplan warns that even as some nations, including the United States, may be retreating into a fortresslike nationalism, this can be only a temporary stage before the world tide of population and poverty forces such prosperous nations to realize that we inhabit one increasingly small and crowded earth.[21]

The one possible exception to this analysis of a rapidly changing, perilously disintegrating world is the oil-exporting region of the Middle East and of Saudi Arabia in particular. In this region, classical, trinitarian, nation-state wars between national armies are still quite possible. But to maintain a Cold War military at the cost of hundreds of billions of dollars annually for the purpose of intervening unilaterally in such a war is the ultimate folly and is premised upon the rejection of superior alternatives. We can develop domestic conventional energy supplies; we can develop alternative, renewable energy supplies; we can expand our pool of foreign suppliers to include, for example, Russia; we can contribute air, sea, and limited land forces to genuine international expeditionary forces intervening in the Middle East; we can, most of all, undertake realistic conservation measures and use energy much more wisely. All these measures represent a viable alternative to maintaining a Cold War standing army whose principle mission is the prospective occupation of Saudi Arabia or other parts of the Middle East in order to continue the supply of cheap oil to us and our oil-importing friends.

In a concluding interview before leaving office, former U.S. Secretary of Energy Hazel O'Leary said that it would take another oil shock to wake the American people to the dangers of dependence on foreign oil: "And that appears about as certain as another hurricane in Florida or earthquake in California. *The only question is when.*"[22]

When religious zealots deposed our most valued ally in the region, the shah of Iran, we were powerless to throw them out, impose a more friendly government, or otherwise exert our will. What makes us think we could do any better in Saudi Arabia? Do we really believe we could occupy Saudi Arabia indefinitely, propping up a puppet government and holding off an irregular army of zealots dispersed throughout the cities and oil fields of the country, blowing up production, refining, and distribution facilities and carrying out a jihad against the occupying forces? The parents of the American troops might suddenly decide that the lives of their sons and daughters were worth more than gasoline at $1.25 per gallon. They might also have some rather harsh questions for their elected officials and military leaders who permitted them for so long to believe otherwise. Or, in the words of a *New York Times* news account:

> Cheap oil is still a boon to the American economy. The G.A.O. [General Accounting Office] put the benefits of cheap oil at hundreds of billions of dollars annually. *Its analysis explicitly excluded the cost of human life in sending American soldiers back into Mideastern oil fields*—or the limits that import dependency may impose on American foreign policy. In the current political climate, though, those costs do not seem to be high on anybody's list.[23]

There are a myriad of options to our present defense policy so firmly rooted in the Cold War. But the *necessary* option is a fundamental reform of our military institutions, doctrines, procurement policies, and force structures. It should be the job of presidents, senators, and congresspersons to pursue this course. Since there does not appear to be much prospect of this, however, one of those rare, historic occasions may have arisen where the people themselves, the ultimate sovereigns in our system, have to rise up and demand a new defense policy for a new era.

Clausewitz was clearly correct about one thing: war is conducted by the government, the army, and the people. Much of the argument presented here has discussed the government and the army. When these institutions are stuck in a rapidly vanishing past, it is up to the third entity, the people, to exert their collective will. It can happen—indeed it must, else we risk humiliating failure and possibly disaster in the next century.

The central theme of Bill Mauldin's classic World War II cartoons was the gap between Willie and Joe—the troops—and the higher-ups—the generals and the politicians. This gap widened by orders of magnitude in the Cold War years with the introduction of scientific and policy wizardry. Military hardware became too complicated for soldiers, let alone civilians, to understand. And the intricate foreign policy chessboards set up in Georgetown salons were clearly beyond the reach of ordinary Americans. As elites have done throughout history, both systems cloak themselves in a language so recondite as to ensure the confusion, and therefore alienation, of ordinary citizens.

But as one who has seen it from both sides, I can confirm that there is nothing—*nothing*—in the whole framework of military policy and practice that any American of ordinary intelligence cannot understand. Concerned citizens—and we all should be concerned—can demand an explanation as to why our forces are structured as they are, why they are equipped one way rather than another, and, most of all, why they should be sent here or there in the world. It boils down to common sense which can be found at least as readily on Main Street as on Pennsylvania Avenue.

The first step in restoring sanity and perspective to U.S. military matters is the reengagement of the American people. If that engagement leads to the re-creation of a citizen military, an army of the people, it will revolutionize our foreign and defense policies and prepare us for a new era. Average Americans will once again have a stake and an immediate interest in virtually every action taken by their president, the chairman of the Joint Chiefs, and the Senate and House Armed Services committees in a way they have not since they laid down their arms in 1945. Should such a revolutionary thing occur, it will be one of the more important events in our nation's history.

Chapter 3

The Mysterious Disappearance of the "Peace Dividend"

The U. S. Army base at Fort Hood, Texas, is, in effect, "the largest corporation in the state of Texas." Including its contracts and payroll, it generates about $2 billion a year in local economic activity.[1] Albeit massive, Fort Hood is simply one of several tips of the iceberg. Consider the following U. S. force structures seven years after the demise of our only serious threat:

- U. S. Army: 482,800 men and women in active service, plus 595,100 in the Reserve and Guard, equals 1,077,900 personnel; 10,497 main battle tanks; 31,477 armored vehicles; 8,160 artillery pieces; 5,331 helicopters.
- U. S. Navy: 395,600 active-duty personnel, plus 231,500 in the Naval Reserve, equals 627,100 total naval personnel; 144 surface combatants; 99 submarines; 736 surface support ships; 3,020 fixed-wing aircraft; 1,403 helicopters.
- U. S. Air Force: 378,700 airmen and -women, plus

182,500 in the Reserve and Guard, for a total personnel of 561,200; 174 long-range strike bombers; 3,750 tactical aircraft; 1,113 transport aircraft; 2,209 support aircraft; 218 helicopters;

- U. S. Marine Corps: 174,900 men and women, plus 42,100 reserves, for a total of 217,000 personnel; 2,365 armored vehicles; 619 fixed-wing aircraft; 728 helicopters (both of the latter are in the Navy inventory); and a wide array of rocket and other weaponry.[2]

Personnel totals now are approximately 1.5 million in regular or active-duty status and just over 1 million in reserve or National Guard status. Thus, the United States on the eve of the twenty-first century possesses a military force of more than 2.5 million people and no serious identifiable threat to our security.

This vast inventory, almost too great to comprehend, represents two things: the greatest fighting force in the history of the world; and one of the greatest military anomalies in human history. "America is experiencing a deep confusion of purpose at this moment in history, holding onto a past that is defunct but unable to imagine a different future," says one civilian analyst.[3] Rather than seek to imagine a different future, the current administration proposes to spend $30 billion more than the current annual defense budget of $250 billion and to increase weapons procurement by 48 percent over the next five years. The Republican Party proposes even greater increases. Much of the vast weapons inventory purchased with budget-busting deficits in the gargantuan military buildup of the 1980s is now being sold or given to foreign nations, such as Brazil, Bahrain, and Bosnia, or dumped in the ocean to form artificial reefs, in order to make room for newer, more sophisticated replacements only a decade later.

With the vivid exceptions of Korea and Vietnam, the Cold War was largely a covert war, a struggle carried out in secret. The sacred rites and mysteries of the priesthood of espionage, the technological wizardry of weaponry, and the recondite rules of Great Power gamesmanship were all used to insulate the Court of Washington from the Country of America. By and large, the role of the American citizen-taxpayer was to pick up the bill. And we the taxpayers had every right to believe that, if we were ever successful in "the long twilight struggle" against Communism, things would be different at the other end of the interminable tunnel. Well, we were successful, but things aren't different.

A cycle of economic boom has masked the continued Cold War–level costs of a somewhat reduced (but not reshaped) military. Perversely, part of the economic boom is fueled by continued procurement of dubious weapons. But few are inclined to question the number of scholarships a canceled B-2 bomber might provide, the cancer research to be carried out for the price of a Nimitz-class aircraft carrier, the toxic and nuclear waste cleanup financed by the postponement of even a portion of "Star Wars" research and development.

Taxpaying citizens will not rise up against misguided defense priorities until the economy slackens and retreats or until entitlement costs soar in the early twenty-first century. Then federal revenues will fail to cover the cost of middle-class social programs and wholesale cuts in military budgets will be demanded. Sadly, after the cleaver falls, all that will remain is a Cold War military body with certain extremities lopped off.

In 1997, the Department of Defense carried out its regular Quadrennial Defense Review (QDR), for periodic assessment of the correlation between military capability and security threats. Critical consensus concluded that the QDR contributed little to post–Cold War military thinking, settling instead for rubber-stamp ratification of the status quo— namely, maintenance of a Cold War military structure designed to prosecute two major regional conflicts. Given the makeup of the QDR panel, few were surprised at this outcome. Its seven principal panels included at least seven flag-rank military officers, and representatives of the defense industry participated in subpanels. True to fashion, the military establishment concluded that it was doing pretty well. Full speed ahead.

Anticipating this outcome, a few members of Congress successfully argued for the creation of a National Defense Panel (NDP) to provide an independent assessment of military needs. Since the majority of the NDP members were retired military officers and representatives of established think tanks, few reformers expected much fresh, unconventional, or iconoclastic thinking from the NDP report issued in December, 1997. To the surprise of many, however, the NDP concluded: "the challenges of the twenty-first century will be quantitatively and qualitatively different from those of the Cold War and require fundamental change to our national security institutions, military strategy, and defense posture by 2020." The Panel recommended a "transformation strategy" that recognizes the urbanization of warfare; the need for lighter, faster, smaller, and more mobile force structures; new operational concepts; and greater integration of reserves into the total force because "these citizen-soldiers ensure the involvement of the American people in our nation's security."

Historically, however, it has been the rule that a closed military system will rarely reform itself absent serious outside pressure or, more tragically, a major military defeat.

For those concerned to create the former in order to prevent the latter, it is necessary first to ask basic questions: What current forces do we have and how are they structured? Is our present system for equipping and maintaining these forces financially and politically sound? Are the contingencies to which our forces are preparing to respond the most likely to happen, and do they represent the greatest danger to our society? These are the questions that should be, but are not being, asked by an equally closed political system in Washington. For, how can we expect politicians unable to reform themselves to reform the Pentagon?

U.S. military forces, especially the Army, have been reduced since the end of the Cold War. The so-called "Base Force" review at the end of the Cold War resulted in a reduction from sixteen Army divisions, representing 770,000 active-duty soldiers and 776,000 drilling reservists, to twelve divisions in 1993 and, pursuant to the so-called Bottom-Up Review, to ten divisions thereafter. The second reduction was largely achieved by replacing National Guard round-out brigades with active-duty brigades from eliminated divisions.

Regular Army combat divisions are deployed as follows: two divisions under European Command in Germany; two divisions under Pacific Command in Hawaii; six divisions representing contingency forces deployed under four separate commands in the continental United States. There are fourteen combat division equivalents in the reserve forces, focused on fifteen National Guard "enhanced readiness brigades," under state National Guard headquarters and an Army Reserve Force Command in Georgia.

It is worthwhile briefly to revisit the short, thorny history of the "Total Force" concept, and especially its central feature, the "round-out" brigades, to appreciate fully the continuing complex relationship between regular and reserve forces and the political backdrop against which it is played out. One of the several clichéd "lessons of Vietnam," confirmed perhaps more for the military than for politicians, was: "Don't go to war unless the people are behind you." This led civilian and military commanders in the Pentagon in 1973 to devise the Total Force idea, designed to integrate regular and reserve forces as a means of requiring the commander-in-chief to mobilize local public sentiment in support of a proposed military expedition. The Total Force concept included "round out" brigades of National Guards and was based on the theory that political leadership would be required to explain the national security interest that would justify disruption of individual lives, families, and communities caused by the call-up of the National Guard and reserves as opposed to the relatively simple dispatch of an already-mobilized standing army. During Vietnam, Army generals became convinced that a failure to mobilize the reserves was the primary reason that two successive administrations were able to let it drag on without resolution. Therefore, when President Bush wanted to commit major ground forces in the Persian Gulf in 1990, the Total Force structure required a major reserve call-up, resulting in public interest and support from many towns across the

United States. Interest there certainly was, but public support was less than uniform as evidenced by sharply divided votes in Congress. Quick termination of conflict and low casualty rates prevented the kind of public outcry that most certainly would have accompanied a prolonged, bloody conflict (i.e., "Vietnam in the desert"). Nevertheless, the principal point remains: integration of regular and reserve forces requires significantly more political leadership in public persuasion of the national urgency necessitating reserve mobilization.

The Army's response to the force reductions from sixteen to twelve and eventually ten active-duty combat divisions following the Persian Gulf War and the end of the Cold War, however, was to discard the round-out National Guard brigades in favor of preserving the numbers of regulars in the remaining active divisions. Not unexpectedly, the Army justified discarding the Guard brigades on grounds of their low readiness and marginal preparedness during the Persian Gulf call-up. These judgments are hotly disputed by National Guard officials, who claim much higher readiness status of Guard brigades than the Regular Army was willing to admit and who claim, with considerable justification, that any Guard deficiencies in training and equipment were directly traceable to Regular Army neglect.[4]

Interestingly, the Army has found occasion since the Persian Gulf conflict to revive the Total Force concept as a political hedge. It chose to mobilize 2,000 reservists as part of its 20,000-troop commitment to peacekeeping in Bosnia. These token forces operate as a trip wire as the U.S. presence in Bosnia lingers beyond its deadline and if conflict erupts. A broader reserve call-up can be requested by the Army as a means of testing public and congressional resolve for a political mission that has little public appeal. Thus, the Army can use reserve mobilization policy as a hedge against missions it may not favor and refuse to activate reserves for missions where it wishes to emphasize the need for a large permanent standing army and discredit the professional capability of the National Guard and reserves.

The proposition being tested here is whether the likely military missions of the future might better be carried out by a substantially smaller standing army augmented by a better-trained and equipped, highly mobile and ready reserve force (and which missions, requiring call-up of the Guard, should be carried out at all). Part of the answer to this question rests on the relative cost effectiveness of the present system versus the proposed system, coupled with a clearer definition of future threats. On the matter of the present and projected costs of maintaining a Cold War army in the post–Cold War era, the facts are neither encouraging nor wholesome.

Over the decades of the Cold War, and beyond, considerable effort has been made by Pentagon analysts and critics to rationalize what otherwise seems to be an irrational monster called the Pentagon budget. The basic questions are: how much needs to be spent to defend the United States, and is that amount being spent wisely and well? The annual defense budget is a composite of requests from the Army, the Air Force, and the Navy, whose budget also includes that of the Marine Corps. The budget of the U.S. Coast Guard, which is part of the defense establishment during wartime, is contained in the overall budget of the Department of Transportation. Multibillion-dollar nuclear weapons development programs are included in the budget of the Department of Energy. And tens of billions of dollars required by an elaborate intelligence establishment, and forming an integral part of national defense, are likewise separate from the Department of Defense budget. Thus, total costs of national security run close to $50 billion annually *above* the current Department of Defense budget of approximately $250 billion or more.

Once the individual services submit their annual budget requests through the individual service secretaries and the Joint Chiefs of Staff to the secretary of defense, the total Defense Department budget then goes through the administration's Office of Management and Budget and from the White House to the Congress. There, defense committees of the Senate and the House of Representatives review, analyze, and at least marginally alter the budget before it is finally approved by the full membership of both Houses. This ritual is both intricate and elaborate, often involving intense debate on this or that weapons system, with defenders of a particular system more often than not representing those interest groups benefiting most from its development and production. These same substantial economic interests too often also cause members of Congress or congressional delegations to push for procurement of weapons not requested by the services or the Defense Department. Since virtually all weapons procurement decisions represent major public works jobs programs, whatever else they may represent for national defense, competition among weapons contractors and among states and districts is as intense as any in Washington.

Although it is not our purpose to debate the pros and cons of defense budgeting, a proposal for a new citizen-based military, an army of the people, cannot neglect the procedures used to finance today's standing Cold War army. Few serious analysts of our current defense budgeting system believe it produces the most effective defense in the most efficient way, especially since the United States presently accounts for about 37 percent of the world's defense expenditures. When the expenditures of our allies and other nonthreatening nations are added, that figure rises to 67 percent. By comparison, Russia's disintegrating national defense system represents about 10 percent of global defense expenditures, China about 1 percent, and all of what are called the "rogue states" (Libya, Syria, Iraq, North Korea, etc.) about 2 percent. These substantial spending disparities prevail even after U. S. combat forces have been reduced in the post–Cold War 1990s by 30 percent or more. For example, Army active-duty maneuver battalions have been reduced more than 40 percent, the Navy fleet by some 37 percent, and Air Force tactical fighter wings by almost 50 percent.

There are few analysts more thoughtful or trenchant in their criticisms of current Defense Department budgeting practices than Charles Spinney, who has spent almost a quarter-century examining Pentagon—especially Air Force—budgets. As with any outspoken critic accustomed to escalating rhetoric and occasionally raising decibels to force attention to strongly held, but often unexamined beliefs, Spinney's views have offended many. However, one does not have to agree with every assertion to take a point where it is well made and factually defended. "Defense spending, like entitlements," claims Spinney, "is now poised to explode over the long term," despite force reductions. Spinney notes with irony that, on November

14, 1995, the day President Clinton and House Speaker Gingrich closed down all "non-essential operations" of the U.S. government for the first time, the director of the Defense Finance and Accounting Service, Mr. Richard Keevey, reported to a congressional committee that financial managers in the Pentagon could not audit their books. Keevey rated the ability to track where defense dollars flow as a three on a scale of ten. Auditors from Congress's investigatory arm, the General Accounting Office, confirmed Keevey's assessment, reporting that at least $20 billion of expenditures could not be matched to items they purportedly purchased. Agreeing with both assessments, the Defense Department's own inspector general assigned seven hundred auditors to clean up the accounting mess, but testified to the congressional panel that rationality could not be expected in chaotic defense expenditures before the year 2000. Spinney concludes that if the Pentagon cannot audit its own books, it is not accountable to or controlled by the people. So, in terms of accountability, defense spending does not meet the minimum standard of constitutional performance for public institutions or accepted business practice for private ones.

To summarize the fiscal state of post–Cold War defenses: first, including intelligence collection and analysis, nuclear weapons research and development, and coastal defenses, total defense-related spending is well over $300 billion annually; second, the Communist threat, our principal Cold War concern, has collapsed; third, the United States, its allies, and benign states account for over two-thirds of all world military spending; fourth, actual U. S. combat forces have been reduced on average by 30 percent; and fifth, Department of Defense accounting procedures are in a state of disrepair if not chaos. On top of all this, the Joint Chiefs of Staff are seeking to accelerate the rate of spending growth. There can be only one reason for this demand for increased spending given the foregoing circumstances: "The *costs* of the new weapons entering the inventories are going through the roof."[5] In other words, the costs of individual weapons, whether aircraft, tanks, ships, helicopters, or artillery pieces, is growing faster than the total expenditures or budgets for these weapons.

Spinney uses airplanes, his specialty, to prove a point that is applicable to a host of other military procurement items. He notes that the Air Force's long-term acquisition plans will produce 56 percent *fewer* airplanes, or 792 aircraft versus 1,800 today. This is true because the average cost per plane in the first decade of the twenty-first century will be $86.7 million or 210 percent *more* than the $28-million-per-plane average between 1983 and 1992. This represents an accelerating trend. In the first decade of the Cold War, the United States procured 7,688 planes at a cost of about $47 billion, and in the last decade of the Cold War it bought 1,800 new airplanes at a cost of $50.3 billion. This represents a 77 percent production *decline* in overall numbers of aircraft. Even given dramatically increased technological sophistication, at some point numbers matter. Few would advocate that the United States should entrust its defenses to a handful of technologically superior aircraft. Aside from increased budget requests, the Air Force's answer to number shrinkage is age growth: it proposes to permit the average age of combat fighter airplanes to leap from 9.6 years in 1996 to a record high of 19.2 years in 2006. Even in a perfect world, Spinney calculates this means retiring fighter aircraft at 40 to 42 years of service life. "This would be, by far, the most extreme retirement policy since the dawn of fighter aviation in 1914," he says. The same trend toward fewer numbers and older equipment applies to almost all categories of military hardware. According to Spinney, "With a few exceptions, the average age of our equipment would be older in the mid-1990s than it was in the 1980s, and this smaller force would be flown, marched, steamed, and driven less often than in the 1980s."

Spinney's analysis helps to explain a political puzzle the American people have inexplicably left unsolved: Since the Cold War is over, why are things going on pretty much the same? Why has there been no peace dividend? The answer is known to all in the defense establishment in Washington but is not discussed openly or candidly with the American people. The post–Cold War high-technology military of fewer numbers and older hardware will require a continuing Cold War budget to maintain. In the one post–Cold War conflict, the Persian Gulf War, even a Cold War budget was insufficient. The United States found it necessary to collect well over $30 billion (some estimates run as high as $100 billion) from its friends and allies to pay part of the costs of fighting a war ostensibly for "democracy in Kuwait" but in truth for continued access to relatively inexpensive oil from Kuwait and the Gulf region. Since precedents did not exist in U.S. law for renting the American military to foreign countries, Congress was forced to create something called the Defense Cooperation Fund, which received the contributions from grateful oil-importing nations and from which Congress "appropriated" funds to fight the war. "Cynics might conclude from these bizarre activities that the United States is exporting troops to earn hard currency," wrote Spinney in 1990. "Is the all-volunteer army becoming the source of the 20th century Hessians or Janissaries?"[6] Any person with common sense confronted with these facts and the straightforward dictionary definition of a mercenary as a "professional soldier hired by a foreign country" would have to answer in the affirmative. It is equally safe to conclude that an army of the people would not have permitted its political leaders to rent it out so easily.

The nexus of budget, politics, and standing military must be explored further to understand its perverse implications and to appreciate why only a different kind of military, a true citizen army, can break the cycle of increasingly expensive defense decay. A former secretary of the navy, John Lehman, provides one part of the mosaic. "It's too late to stop the buildup to a 600-ship navy," he gloated in December 1982. "We've already accomplished it, because we front-loaded the budget." "Front-loading" is a political term of art for spending early-year appropriations for a multiyear procurement—usually of a capital investment item such as an aircraft carrier or bomber or submarine—on key components such as keels or engines so that, as costs first grow, then soar, it becomes more expensive to terminate the weapons program than to complete it.

Front-loading has a twin in the defense power game that Spinney calls political engineering, a shorthand phrase for an elaborate, well-established, sophisticated Cold War procedure of spreading parts of weapons systems into as many states and congressional districts as possible. Needless to say, contracts that create jobs in local communities are beneficial to the politicians who obtain them and constituents who receive them, thus generating widespread political support for weapons systems whether needed for security or not and whether cost-effective or not. As one illustration, a new-generation fighter aircraft, the F-22, has produced research and development contracts and subcontracts for 1,150 companies employing 15,000 people in 43 states and Puerto Rico. In full production, the F-22 will create 160,000 jobs. Between 1989 and 1995, pieces of the B-2 bomber were being produced in 383 congressional districts in 46 states by 3,000 contractors employing 53,000 workers. The SSN-21 submarine was built in 44 states. Pieces of the F-15E fighter come from 46 states. The F-16 fighter involves 3,216 contractors in 390 congressional districts in 46 states. The C-17 transport aircraft is produced by more than 2,000 contractors bringing $4.5 billion to local economies. Overall, the spectacular 1980s military buildup increased government-dependent jobs in the private sector by 1.4 million jobs or by 84 percent. Although this form of public works job program is probably the least cost-effective in terms of numbers of jobs created per dollar spent, it is highly favored politically because the jobs are performed in the nominally private sector and because they are justified as necessary to give America a "strong defense."

So highly favored are these defense power games that, despite the disappearance of the Cold War threat, Congress *added* almost $7 billion to the fiscal year 1996 defense budget and is expected to *add* almost $13 billion in fiscal year 1997 *beyond* the Pentagon's request. Needless to say, little of these add-ons will go for training, operations, or readiness; almost all will go for development or procurement of hardware, much of which the military has not requested. Spinney says that the

Pentagon and its willing partner, the Congress, have been playing these games (front-loading and political engineering) with
increasing subtlety for the last thirty-five years. During peacetime, both sides benefit. Pentagonians gain money and power,
and congressional incumbents get pork and votes. But these
games sacrifice the real needs of the military on the altar of
pork-barrel politics, and they guarantee costs will grow faster
than budgets, even when budgets grow at very high rates.
Front-loading and political engineering encourage immoral
behavior at all levels within the Defense Department by making money, not genuine national security, the focus of decisions. We exaggerate the threat to justify larger budgets and
use deceitful if not illegal accounting tricks to hide the true
costs of programs. Finally, Spinney says, by addicting specific
regions and their representatives in Congress to the narcotic of
defense spending, these political games corrupt the relationship between the Defense Department and Congress.[7]

One does not have to share all of Spinney's conclusions to
see that the net effect of a cynical political system is to start a
money flow which, because of its widespread distribution, is
virtually impossible to stop. From a strictly budgetary stand-
point, this is insidious. But this labyrinthine arrangement also
ensures a less than healthy addiction of consumer-constituents
to economic stimulation created by unproductive investment
in weapons. Finally and most perniciously, it subverts the constitutional system of checks and balances, based in part on
congressional oversight, which is necessary to the proper func-
tioning of the American democracy. Indeed, according to critics such as Spinney, the very purpose of late-twentieth-century
weapons procurement is to transfer the power of the purse

from Congress to the executive branch of government, thus corrupting the balance of power the Founding Fathers established in the Constitution. The primitive fear and secrecy engendered by the Cold War hid the base political nature of these games.[8]

If the exigencies of the Cold War excused much extraconstitutional abuse, its end must become the occasion for reforming a system in which abuse is endemic. The best way to break the Congress-contractor-constituency cycle is through an army of the people. Citizen-taxpayer-soldiers will be the first to spot and protest procurement abuse. Citizens faced with the prospect of combat using fewer, older weapons will be the first to complain of a system that produced them. The members of a standing military, concerned with promotion and career like their counterparts in the Congress, are much less likely to question a system upon which their day-to-day livelihood is dependent. This is simple human nature. As a matter of public policy, the proposal for a citizen army stands apart from reform of the procurement system. But as a practical matter, the two are inseparable.

Politically, the greatest therapeutic benefit of a citizen army would be the large-scale reengagement of taxpaying citizens in issues of national defense and security. The veil of Cold War secrecy, so often dropped on "national security" grounds, can no longer justify shrouding weapons procurement and deployment-of-forces issues. Issues of national defense should no longer be the recondite reserve of the policy elites and uniformed military in Washington. "War is too serious a matter to entrust exclusively to military men," should be the watchword, and it is much too serious to be entrusted to pork-barreling members of Congress. The Cold War pattern continues long after the Cold War in a mindless pattern unquestioned by presidents and national leaders. Investments in new weapons routinely exceed budget projections. Force sizes and numbers of weapons decrease because technological sophistication escalates unit costs. Modernization rates decrease as individual unit age increases. Readiness—the ability to fight and win, tomorrow if necessary—should no longer be sacrificed to procurement, nor should citizen-soldiers tolerate that sacrifice. Anyone who spends time in the esoteric world of defense and security readily relates to Spinney's pointed, commonsense question: "If readiness is truly the top priority, then why do senior [defense] decision-makers expend far more effort and time on acquisition decisions than on operations and maintenance or sustainability decisions?"[9]

A considerable number of respected defense pathologists have been brought to drastic conclusions from years of observation of extrademocratic behavior in the military establishment. A repetitive pattern of wildly optimistic budget numbers, chaotic accounting practices, and total failure of political accountability leads inexorably to this conclusion: "The Department of Defense's tolerance of misleading accounting information suggests the presence of hidden anti-democratic agendas or incompetence or both. . . . Degenerate accounting practices are more consistent with the pathologies of socialism (i.e., central planning, top-down management, negotiated prices, cost-plus economics, game playing, bureaucratic logrolling, deal-making, etc.) than with the self-correcting behavior induced by the free play of a competitive market."[10]

In response to our current flawed defense system, a series

of "shock therapy" steps based upon the fundamentals required to restore coherence and integrity must be adopted. First, all witnesses before congressional military committees from the secretary of defense on down should testify under oath.[11] Second, Congress should be required to pass a joint national threat-assessment resolution every two years explicitly analyzing its views of dangers facing America. Third, the five-year Defense Plan, the Pentagon's master plan, should be declassified and submitted to Congress and the American people; little, if any, of its contents require classification, a traditional measure for limiting public debate. Fourth, Congress should establish a politically independent Defense Evaluation Board tasked with eliminating front-loading, political engineering, and bureaucratic logrolling. Finally, the Pentagon should be required to adopt standard commercial, industrial, and engineering cost estimating, as well as work measurement and performance practices.

These measures are meant to force greater congressional involvement and accountability both on the Defense Department and on Congress itself. Adding increased national dependence on a strong citizen military would dramatically increase such accountability. Drawing the bulk of national defense forces directly from the people would greatly strengthen citizen awareness of and involvement in issues of national security. With an army of the people, the people would hold their representatives in Congress more accountable for their performance, or nonperformance, in defense matters. Paradoxically enough, a citizen army *could* even cause citizens themselves to question their own acquiescence in a weapons procurement process that rewards elected representatives for trading votes-for-weapons-for-jobs, a system having less to do with national defense and more to do with political logrolling.[12]

At present, the United States is defended by a military establishment designed, structured, and equipped to counter a Warsaw Pact invasion of central Europe. In the decade of the 1990s, that establishment has been modestly reduced in size and redirected toward the possibility of fighting two major regional conflicts (MRCs) simultaneously. The military brain has begun to struggle with a different mode of thinking. But the body, while slightly smaller, still looks the same, that of the permanent professional, and the armor it puts on itself still looks very much the same as before. That armor has more expensive technological trinkets, but it is procured through a system that is increasingly cynical and corrupting.

As William Lind, a lifelong military reformer (and co-author of *America Can Win: The Case for Military Reform*), recently said: "The Pentagon is no longer the military headquarters of a superpower—it is a bank. An annual defense budget, not an army and navy, is its principal product. The Pentagon has become merely a trough for contractors and Congressmen, not the vital center of national strategy and defense."[13]

Even if the United States returns to a citizen military, an army of the people, that step would not cure all present ills, such as outdated strategies, tactics, and doctrines, misguided threat assessments, and politically manipulated weapons procurement procedures. But citizen-soldiers would, at the very least, engage themselves, their families, and their communities in arenas too long open only to defense professionals and national security elites. An environment of common sense, distinctly uncomfortable to those accustomed to business as usual, would be created. The simple act of creating that environment, of engaging ordinary citizens in matters relating to their defense, would make America more secure than all the Seawolf submarines, F-22 fighter aircraft, and Aegis destroyers we can buy.

Given our inclination to take our own history for granted and therefore to leave it unexamined, we Americans assume the Army we have is the Army we have always had, that little if any alternative to a large, expensive, standing military exists. Too few know that almost three thousand years of republican history warn against such an institution, that permanent armies have consistently been seen as antithetical to democracies, or that the debate over professional military versus citizen militia was one of the fiercest in American constitutional history. The argument made here for restoration of an army of the people is rooted in this rich republican history, tradition, and philosophy. Therefore, before offering the components of such an army for the next century, its foundation in history should be explored.

Chapter 4

The Republic and the Militia

The notion of the citizen-soldier has a tradition strongly rooted in colonial, prerevolutionary America and, in more ancient times, in the Greek city-state and the earliest Greek and, later, Roman republics. In revolutionary America, the Minuteman—young, mobile, citizen-guerrilla—took on heroic qualities that eventually assumed mythic proportions. He has fought in every American war. As an individual, he is never an instrument of the state, but rather he is the guarantor of his own freedom. He is Sergeant York, William Holden in *The Bridges of Toko-Ri,* and even Luke Skywalker. He does not belong to the Army. He belongs to the ideal of America.

Ever individualists, the early Americans resisted central authority in military matters as well as in other aspects of public life. Strongly motivated by radical Whig ideology, which depicted standing armies as instruments of tyranny, they saw the militia as the proper recourse for republican citizens seeking to defend their political liberties, their property, and ultimately their freedom.[1] One historian of the period notes that provincial soldiers, whether volunteers or conscripts, were citizens first and soldiers second.[2] Because of resentment by provincial soldiers toward central authority, represented either by colonial governments or the British army, prerevolutionary society was intensely local. In military affairs, soldiers identified closely with local units and officers and insisted on explicit contractual recognition of their personal rights. Instead of the mythological, Turnerian frontier citizen-soldiery, transformed by contact with Native Americans and the New World's forests, modern historians examining prerevolutionary America found a complex military system with institutional similarities to the English militia, which itself was tied closely to town and country life. In this system, the militia fulfilled social and political functions as well as military needs. By 1700, the militia had become an established colonial institution. Virtually all colonies required some type of universal military training and service for eligible men. Militiamen were also required to arm and equip themselves.[3]

Although time, economic exigencies, and the Revolution itself eroded the purity of the militia ideal, the militia principle was well established in American society. On the eve of the Revolution, the Americans carried with them over a century and a half of military experience which began with a universal military obligation eventually modified by economic necessity and political opposition. An inclusive militia system that imposed service on all classes in the colonies had given way to a system that preferred to use "marginal men" whenever possible. But Radical Whig republicanism reemerged as the Revolution approached and reasserted a universal military requirement for loyal citizens. Nevertheless, the legacy of colonial history stressed "the new-born states as the focal point of mobilization, a distrust of central authority and strong preference for local control, a deep distaste for military conscription, and a military informality resistant to strict discipline, stark separation of officers and men, and professionalism generally."[4]

Whence did ideas such as civic duty, citizen-soldiers, the militia principle, and local military control originally arise? Seventeenth- and eighteenth-century English militia tradition and radical Whig republicanism have already been suggested as early influences. But these traditions and principles had deeper roots in the ancient Greek polis, the city-state from which the Roman, Renaissance, Enlightenment, and modern republics spring.

In many Greek city-states, ownership of land was a prerequisite for full citizenship, and full citizenship involved frequent military service. Therefore, a close connection developed between agriculture and warfare, the farmer and the warrior. Warfare was often calibrated to the agricultural seasons. (The fourth-century B.C. general and military historian Xenophon quotes Socrates responding to a question concerning what arts or skills are most important: "Well, should we be ashamed to imitate the king of the Persians? For they say that he considers that the noblest and most necessary arts are those of farming and warfare and he practices both most assiduously.")

Trespass by invading warriors on the land of the Greek farmer was sufficient to sound the battle alarm. The very threat of attack on farmland sent phalanxes of heavily armed citizen-farmer-soldiers out to a mutually accepted small plain where a "brief but brutal battle" between invaders and defenders took place. All citizens of the polis were defenders of the inviolability of the small farms and the integrity of the land against invasion. According to Victor Hanson, "Greek hoplite battles were struggles between small landholders who by mutual consent sought to limit warfare (and hence killing) to a single, brief, nightmarish occasion." When later city-states undertook to abandon the land under attack and withdraw within the city walls, warfare then became continuous, relentless, and prolonged, and "the entire notion that infantry battle was integrated irrevocably with agriculture was cast aside."[5]

Athenian citizens were eligible for military service between the ages of eighteen and forty-two. Those citizens between the ages of eighteen and twenty took an oath and served as *ephebes* (plebes or recruits). They were given military and civic training in their first year of service; during this first year, they served as well on guard duty at the port of Athens. In their second year, they received the shield and spear of a hoplite (so called after the *hoplon,* the great shield born by these phalanx warriors) at state expense. They then served on garrison duty on the Athenian frontiers. After this period, they joined the regular body of citizens. This system provides an excellent early example of the direct connection between citizenship and military service.[6]

As a number of classical scholars point out, community or citizen militias rather than a standing or paid army guaranteed the safety and freedom of the community at large. Classical scholars conclude that it was not the case that all Greeks were purely soldiers. The Greek male, even if he was at certain times a soldier, was also typically a farmer, a craftsman, or both.[7] All male Greek citizens being subject to some kind of military service, the notion of the warrior defending the state was inseparable from the citizen serving as soldier. Service as a soldier was seen as a fulfillment of citizenship and an honored privilege. Self-sacrifice for the common good, more than personal excellence in battle, was held to be the principal goal. This ideal of common effort produced a constant emphasis on remaining at one's post for the common good. The success of the phalanx was dependent militarily on steadfastness at one's post. Subordination of individual glory to the common good was a belief system in support of practical necessity. "Individual courage and success matter as profoundly as they did in the world of Homer, but now they are displayed as part of a common effort."[8]

That matters of military and "foreign" policy were not segregated by the leaders from the citizens at large is amply demonstrated by Thucydides' account of the extensive debate among the Athenians over their proposed conquest of Sicily in the period between the winter of 416 and the summer of 413 B.C. In the second of two citizen assemblies held within five days, the Athenians voted "full powers" to the generals Alcibiades, Nicias, and Lamachus to organize a considerable infantry and naval force to order matters in Sicily as they should deem best "in the interests of Athens." In the assembly, Nicias argued against the expedition on the grounds that the Sicilians "would fear us most if we never went there at all" . . . and that "at the least reverse to us they would at once begin to look down upon us, and would join our enemies here [in Attica] against us." Against Nicias, and for conquest, Alcibiades argued the case of hegemony: ". . . we cannot fix the exact point at which our empire shall stop; we have reached a position in which we must not be content with retaining what we have but must scheme to extend it for, if we cease to rule others, we shall be in danger of being ruled ourselves."

The party of war prevailed, but after a time, as the history of the Peloponnesian War shows, the siege of the city of Syracuse dragged on, matters in Sicily deteriorated badly, and the Athenians continued to do battle with occupying Peloponnesian forces in Attica. Predictably, "heavy charges fell upon them, produced their financial distress" and they "imposed upon their subjects, instead of the tribute, the tax of a twentieth upon all imports and exports by sea, which they thought would raise more money" for the dual war effort. Eventually, the Sicilian expedition concluded in a military and economic disaster for the Athenians, who would not heed Nicias' wise counsel.[9]

These same war years established further principles concerning the democratization of military affairs. A struggle between the forces of democracy and the forces of oligarchy, the Four Hundred, in Athens spread to the city of Samos. Athenian prodemocracy military forces in Samos deposed generals and officers of the oligarchy and elected generals who supported their democratic ideals. Similarly, earlier Athenian assemblies had banished some generals and fined others for accepting bribes and making premature peace in an earlier expedition against Sicily.[10]

The ethic of the Greek citizen-soldier was based upon his willingness to make any sacrifice necessary to defend his land, family, community, and the common good. In honoring this credo, few passages in the literature of the praise of valor can compete with the classic funeral oration by Pericles in honor of those who fell in the first year of the prolonged Peloponnesian War:

> It seems to me that the death of these men has provided both a reminder and a final proof of manly courage. . . . They considered it most glorious to undergo danger and to strike at the enemy while relinquishing all else. Success in battle they left in the hands of hope; they trusted in themselves in the face of battle. They considered that it was better to fight and suffer death than to save themselves by flight. So they fled a shameful reputation and endured the physical danger, and in a brief moment of time they were taken away from what was the height of their glory rather than their fear. So were these men worthy of their city.[11]

It was, ironically, the Peloponnesian War that began the erosion of the citizen-soldier concept and the introduction of mercenary warriors. As the war dragged on, the wealth of the state increasingly was used to recruit professional specialists skilled in weapons such as the sling and the bow, which hoplites despised as cowardly. Gradually, the Greeks' ability to moderate the scope and dimension of military contests was lost as professionals assumed command and the concept of total war began to be born. Greek warfare recognized the mercenary as a social type with interests sometimes different from the civilians he defended and even different from the state which employed him.[12]

The Roman experience was similar to that of the Greeks, if less pronounced. The transformation of Rome from early republic to mature empire was accompanied by a parallel transformation of its army. As Rome evolved from the fourth century B.C. to the fourth century A.D., complex interrelationships developed among military service, land ownership, social mobility, and civilian and military worlds.

In its earliest republican years, Rome's military was small, family-based, and relatively unstratified. Early republican political, and especially military, leaders of the fifth and fourth centuries B.C. were characterized more by their resistance to public office than by their lust for it. Foremost among such leaders was Lucius Quinctius Cincinnatus who, having been elected consul of Rome, had to be brought, shedding tears, from behind his plow on "his little farm" to govern the republic. Such leaders in those days "worked with their hands, led frugal lives, did not chafe under honorable poverty, and, far from aiming at positions of royal power, actually refused them when offered." Like all great leaders, Cincinnatus attracted other like-minded citizens, willing to sacrifice for the common good, to positions of responsibility. Among these were Marcus Regulus, who sought leave from military leadership in Africa, somewhat later, to save his farm rather than seek riches from the war; Paulus Emilius, who gave one of his few personal silver pieces to a soldier who had served with distinction in combat; and, notably, Lucius Tarquinius, made master of horse by Cincinnatus, who fought on foot because of his poverty. Dionysius of Halicarnassus ruefully wrote much later that "the

Romans of today do not bear the least resemblance to them." And as for Cincinnatus, he gained even greater fame, once he completed his citizen-consul duties, by hastening to return to the plow.[13]

By the time of the late Republic, on the eve of empire, the rustic republican military led by citizen-soldiers such as Cincinnatus had become a much larger, more cohesive, and more professional army of conquest. Those who were conscripted or volunteered for service in the early Republic did so for specific campaigns, not for a set number of years, and were demobilized thereafter to serve in the military reserves for a period of up to sixteen years. Compared to their later counterparts in the Empire, few soldiers of the Republic benefited from their military service through booty, plunder, or land, because it was much more difficult to build a coherent career in the army of the Republic, which saw itself as a citizens' militia, than in the army of the Empire.[14]

Paralleling the evolution from citizen to professional army was, significantly, the political evolution that accompanied it. In the early to middle Republic, the same procedures were used to assemble the people to vote on war as were used to marshal the army. The Roman people assembled (the *comitia centuriata*) in the Campus Martius to vote on issues of war and peace. If the assembly voted for war, the same venue was then used to organize the military forces. Thus, the ideological link between membership of the citizen body and participation in the armed forces becomes very clear. The point is vividly made by the declining numbers of citizen soldiers between Republic and Empire. An "exceptionally high level" of 26 percent of male citizens participated in the Hannibalic War of the late third century B.C. By the end of the second century B.C., as the army was professionalizing and Rome was moving closer to empire, only 7 to 9 percent participated. So the army of the Republic can be seen as a people's army in numerical as well as ideological terms.

This trend culminated in the creation of a professional standing army as the result of the Augustan reforms. The Roman general Octavian, grandnephew and heir of Caesar and rival of Mark Antony, was a transition figure between Republic and Empire. He prevailed in the Roman civil wars, made himself emperor, and in 27 B.C. became Augustus. He ended the traditional practice of raising citizen forces to fight specific wars and demobilizing them at the end of the conflict. Instead, he replaced the old citizen militia with a new professional army of legions, who served a fixed career term of twenty-five years. Instead of the traditional practice of grants of land for discharged citizen soldiers, Augustus made cash payments to the professional legionnaires funded from new tax levies.

The citizen army of the Republic had provided a vast manpower reserve that had permitted it to surmount even the deepest crisis. The army of the later Empire, though larger in numbers, was unable to stave off the barbarian challenge despite the fact that, since 212 A.D., virtually all imperial subjects enjoyed Roman citizenship. "Yet the Roman state did not turn to them [the citizen base] to make up the military deficit, but instead employed [mercenary] barbarians to fight on its behalf. Now this principle [of the use of citizen-soldiers] was forgotten. In the fifth century [A.D.] the Roman army disappears from view in the West. . . . The Roman state soon follows. *The Roman Empire finally paid the price for Augustus's dissolution of the link between citizenship and military service.*"[15]

There is probably no more vivid illustration in history of the degenerating results of insulating and relieving citizens from public service than the contrast of Rome the Republic with Rome the Empire. The professional, and heavily mercenary, army of the Roman Empire became both the symbol and the instrument of Augustan power centralized in the hands of the emperor and remote from the people. As they no longer were called to serve in it, so they had little voice in its use and misuse. Military matters became of increasing disinterest to them. In the Roman Republic, the sturdiest link of citizen to public affairs was forged by service in its defense. Once that link was weakened, then broken, citizens would have little concern for or interest in affairs on the borders of the Empire. This early division between imperial power and *res publica* prefigured the English Court versus Country and American federalist versus antifederalist debates that were to follow.

In making the transition from ancient Greece and Rome forward to the American constitutional period, it is instructive to consider that scholar of republics who plays such an important role in linking past to present, Niccolò Machiavelli. Though republican to the core, what makes him Machiavelli is his willingness and ability to set those high ideals aside in order to convert a nonrepublican prince to them. He is singularly capable of adopting the most manipulative practices imaginable to the service of his noblest principles. One Florentine patron or another could intemperately imprison him for playing one side off against the other, even though the depth of his ideal-ism in the interest of the republic would scarcely be observed (even today) in the process.

In the service of this republican ideal, no more ardent dis-ciple of the militia principle than Machiavelli exists; and his re-peated and protracted recourse to this issue provides further disproof of his historic role as malevolent cynic. Machiavelli simply could not divorce the role of citizen from the responsi-bility for defense of the republic. Service in the militia became for him the essence of civic virtue. The "well-ordered repub-lic" is his description of a polis governed by a just prince—combining the fierceness of the lion to frighten away the wolves with the shrewdness of the fox in avoiding the snares—and citizens who place the common good at least equal to if not before self-interest. A well-ordered republic is both well trained and well armed, and therefore her character is un-changeable and not dependent on the whims of Fortune. The quality of being well ordered is not simply one of organization; it connotes a republican society that neither despairs in adver-sity nor becomes arrogant in victory. The well-ordered republic is composed of those willing to dedicate their lives, if necessary in combat, to its preservation.

In analyzing Machiavelli's *Art of War (Arte della Guerra),* one scholar claims that his debt to the militia tradition in Flo-rentine theory, plus his experience in actually organizing a mili-tia, leads him to connect citizenship and military virtue to the point where the citizenship actually becomes the product of military service. Resorting to the early Roman republican ideal, Machiavelli believed the citizen should be trained by civic religion and military discipline to devote himself to the patria (nation) and also trained to carry this spirit over into civic affairs. Machiavelli combines his notion of virtue (*virtù*) with Aristotle's ideal of citizen attentiveness to the common good. "The mercenary soldier is a mere instrument in another man's hand; but the citizen-warrior is more than an instrument in the public hand, since his *virtù* is his own and he fights out of knowledge of what he fights for."[16] The citizen-soldier should be what he was in republican Rome where, according to Machiavelli, "the captain, content with triumph, returned to private life with desire; and those who were soldiers put [their] arms down with greater desire than they had picked them up, and each one returned to his trade around which he had arranged [his] life." Here he clearly had the ideal of republican leaders such as Cincinnatus in mind.

Unable to separate citizenship from service in a civilian army or citizen militia, Machiavelli went further. He believed that citizens would fight well only if the city was kept in good order and had just laws, and therefore to commit yourself to a citizen army was necessarily to commit yourself to good laws and a just city. The subtle Florentine, who hated and distrusted mercenaries, argued paradoxically that only a part-time citizen-soldier could be trusted to make full-scale war. "A citizen called to arms, with a home and an occupation of his own, will wish to end the war and go home, where a mercenary, glad rather than sorry if the war drags on indefinitely, will make no attempt to win it." Machiavelli thought that the individual who devoted himself and his energy only to his own business, craft, or trade and not at all to public issues and affairs was less than a citizen and was a weak link in the social chain that bound the city together. Participation in public affairs necessarily and centrally included defense of the city. But one who "makes war his art" (the *condottiere*) is not merely neglecting the good of the city, he is antisocial and makes the duties of citizenship a profession for which he is paid. In the preface to *The Art of War* Machiavelli writes:

> And if, in every other institution of city-states and kingdoms, the greatest care is taken to keep men loyal, peaceable, and full of the fear of God, in the military this care should really be doubled. For in what man can the commonwealth seek greater loyalty than who has promised to die for her? In whom should there be more love of peace than in him who can only be harmed by war? In what man should there be more fear of God than in him who, submitting himself to countless dangers. has greatest need of Him?

Machiavelli is important on the subject of citizen-soldiery not because he is Machiavelli (and at the center of political debate for five hundred years) but because he revived the ideal of citizen participation in governance, an ideal virtually lost since the Greek city-state and the early Roman Republic. This ideal held citizenship to contain duties and responsibilities, the most vital of which was the defense of the country (*patria*). Professional armies removed this duty, thus weakening society and making it more subject to both tyranny and conquest. In *The Prince*, Machiavelli writes: ". . . the arms of another man [mercenary] either slide off your back, weigh you down, or tie you up." A citizen willing to surrender his most important responsibility to a mercenary was likely also to surrender his liberty and freedom. That this question is neither idle nor super-fluous, but indeed is central to the very meaning of republican government, is evidenced by the fact that it recurs in virtually every debate over the nature of republics—including in the American constitutional debate—that has taken place down to the present day.

For American Whigs, the question of citizen versus pro-fessional soldier had already been framed by English political scholars at least a century before. The English civil war of 1642 had provoked a great dispute between the House of Com-mons and Charles I over, among other things, control of the county militia, which the Commons was claiming. Led by Cromwell, the antiroyalist leaders created what was called the New Model Army, which featured, perhaps for the first time, the opportunity for commoners to earn commissions through battlefield valor and the institutionalization of discipline and pay. The New Model Army was one of the first, if not the first, army which belonged to the Commons, and thus to the people. Perversely, however, at the same time, ". . . a military . . . dependency was engrafted upon the commons." For an army, once created, searches incessantly for a branch of government to maintain it. "The professional officer is the cause as well as the effect of this corruption, and his capacity to act in this baneful way arises from the fact that his decision to become a professional has rendered him the lifelong depen-dent of the state that can employ him."[17] And, writes one his-torian, the rank and file fared no better: "The religious impulse which had drawn every man into the [New Model Army] ranks produced a feeling of individual rights, and of spontane-ity of action, which destroyed the dependence of military subordination."[18] Englishmen at home and abroad saw military forces under Cromwell interfere at least six times, usually in the form of abolishment of one parliament or another, in the processes of civil government. Eventually, the New Model Army's excesses—as, for example, its slaughter of the Irish garrison, including women and children, at Drogheda—planted the seeds of a haunting fear of standing armies as a political force and became one of the strongest arguments for the militia system. By the late seventeenth century, the militia came to be seen in England as a means to avoid the corruption of position and centralized power and the instrument for the restoration of freedom, independence, and virtue.

Less than fifteen years later, largely in response to the decline of the Cromwellian Protectorate, which the civil war had produced, James Harrington wrote *The Commonwealth of Oceana,* a utopian political tract that revived Machiavellian republicanism. Harrington resurrected the interrelationship between citizenship and public service in a militia, but with a new dimension. It was crucial, said Harrington, that the citizen-soldier also be a landowner, not merely a tenant or vassal: "It [land ownership] determined whether a man's sword was his lord's or his own and the commonwealth's; and the function of free proprietorship became the liberation of arms, and consequently of the personality, for free public action and civic virtue."[19] If a citizen would fight harder for a just commonwealth than would a mercenary, that citizen would fight harder still if he had a material stake, his own land, in the outcome. The strength of feeling on this issue is evidenced by English political commentators, following Harrington, who regularly coupled a standing army with corruption and privilege:

> A standing Parliament and a standing Army are like those Twins that have their lower parts united, and are divided only above the Navel; they were born together and cannot long outlive each other. The same might be said concerning the only Ancient and true Strength of the Nation, the Legal Militia, and a Standing Army. The Militia must, and can never be otherwise than for English Liberty, because else it does destroy itself; but a standing Force can be for nothing but Prerogative. . . ."[20]

In England in the latter decades of the seventeenth century, the citizen militia became a potent symbol of independent freeholders, republican government, anticorruption, and civic virtue. Following the Revolution of 1688 and the emergence of Britannia as a commercial, military, and imperial power, the division between Court and Country became pronounced, a division presaging the American constitutional debate a century later—and a new debate that should occur in twenty-first-century America. In simplified terms, the Court represented centralized power, the great barons, landed nobility, courtiers and rentiers, the extension of credit for imperial enterprise, and a permanent standing army. The Country, in equally general terms, stood for freeholding citizens, a citizen militia, local authority, and resistance to credit, materialism, and luxury. In the mind of the Country, the Court represented corruption, and the Country represented civic virtue.

Largely from this dispute sprang basic principles such as "separation of powers," later to play such a crucial role in the formation of the American Republic. The central point of the issue in seventeenth-century England was that the party of the Court represented patronage, the promise of office, position, and occasionally pension to members of the Parliament, thus making them courtiers, suborning them to the executive, or the Crown, and corrupting their independence. The Country party, composed largely of independent freeholders, sought to counter this pattern of corruption by proscribing officeholders of the Crown (what were called "placemen") from serving in the Commons and demanding short parliaments, thus requiring members to remain dependent on their constituents rather than on the Court. For the Country party, corruption and centralized power, if backed by a standing army, was the greatest danger to liberty and independence.

The Country argument was well stated at the turn of the eighteenth century by the Scot Andrew Fletcher, described as "a patriot ideologue of high intellectual attainments who would have made an admirable contemporary of Patrick Henry and Richard H. Lee." Anticipating Jefferson, Fletcher was torn between the ideal of an agrarian world of self-sufficient farming warriors and the need for commercial development in impoverished Scotland. He struggled with, but failed to create, a civic morality for market man but prescribed instead military training for all freeholders as a means of education in civic virtue. Fletcher then, after Harrington, added yet another dimension to the mosaic of the predemocratic republic: the citizen-soldier–property owner who is educated in civic virtue—thus, Jefferson's yeoman.

As the struggle continued into eighteenth-century England, other military movements were at work in Europe. Frederick the Great of Prussia, often called the father of the modern army, "pushed warfare in the prevailing code to the limits of acceptable ruthlessness." He was ruthless and rational in his approach to war-making, in keeping with the spirit of the Age of Reason. Because of his professionalization of the Prussian military and the degree to which he made it an instrument of state power—anticipating both Bonaparte and Clausewitz—his Prussian armies established a standard other nations strove to match well into the twentieth century.

By the early eighteenth century in England, Fletcher, like Harrington before and Jefferson later, was being made to seem bucolic at best and irrelevant at worst by the rise of the imperial-commercial-colonial state in the form of Great Britain. For if a nation has empire and commercial domination on its mind, it will first create elaborate, centralized systems of credit, finance, and taxation to provide for the needs of capital and entrepreneurship, and it will form a permanent professional standing army to protect those economic interests and its empire. It will require the system of taxation even more, because a standing army can be a very expensive thing. And it is the very subject of taxation and the British army which it supported that brings us to the doorstep of the American Revolution.

One of the many ironies of the American Revolution was that the militia—a British import from earliest colonial times—was part of the force that defeated the British. This militia heritage, together with the sense of military insecurity and the inability of the economically poor colonies to maintain an expensive professional army, all combined to guarantee that the Elizabethan militia would be transplanted to the North American wilderness. The militia was as complex as any colonial institution. Some aspects of the militia were common to all colonies, while in other respects each colony imprinted its own peculiar identity and culture on its militia as it evolved across generations.[21]

The core of the colonial militia system was universal military commitment for all able-bodied men. This obligation was ensured by colonial laws that simply declared that able-bodied males were members of the militia. The lower age limit varied from sixteen to twenty-one and the upper limit varied from forty-five to sixty. A diverse and eventually expanding list of occupational exemptions from militia service gradually evolved. Militiamen were expected to provide and maintain their own weapons and participate in periodic musters, which were frequent in early colonial times and were gradually reduced to approximately four a year by the beginning of the eighteenth century. Like the political leadership, militia officers were drawn from the colonial establishment, and simultaneous occupation of political office and military command was not uncommon among the upper classes.[22]

As all Americans know, early hostilities against the British in the spring and summer of 1775 were undertaken by various configurations of local militia. When Washington's army largely melted away that summer, he had to liquidate what remained of that army and recruit another while the enemy was within musket range. His only recourse in doing so was to rely on militiamen to fill the gaps until new Continental recruits arrived. Throughout the Revolutionary War, the Continental Army was constantly augmented by colonial militias, thus establishing the "two army" tradition in America. Colonial assemblies revitalized their militias even before the early skirmishes at Concord and Lexington, requiring stiffer training standards, creating weapons and ammunition arsenals, and punishing malingerers. The decentralized nature of the militias democratized and nationalized warfare: "Military authority no longer resided in a sovereign, but in the people and their chosen representatives." Despite Washington's ambiguities concerning the militias' effectiveness, militiamen early on penned Gage's forces inside Boston; later, under the leadership of Ethan Allen, overwhelmed the British garrison at Ticonderoga; then annihilated a Burgoyne detachment outside Bennington, Vermont; and fought splendidly under Greene in the Carolinas, among other accomplishments.[23]

Having successfully prosecuted a war against England using a Continental Army based upon and supported by citizen militia (the image of the Minuteman carries with it a powerful mythic resonance to this day), the founders of the Republic and the drafters of the Constitution were forced to face a dilemma as ancient as the republican ideal itself: shall we have a standing army or citizen militia and, if a standing army, what is its mission? As a great authority on this issue states:

> . . . the Second Amendment to the Constitution, apparently drafted to reassure men's minds against the fact that the federal government would maintain something in the nature of a professional army, affirms the relation between a popular militia and popular freedom in language descended from that of Machiavelli [a shock to the gun lobby, to be sure], which remains a potent ritual in the United States to this day. The new

republic feared corruption by a professional army, even while—like England a century before—it saw no alternative to establishing one; and the implications of the rhetoric employed in this context were to be fully worked out in the debates and journalism of the first great conflict between American parties.[24]

Among those whose views affected preconstitutional thinking in colonial America was the legal scholar William Blackstone. According to Blackstone, "In free states . . . no man should take up arms but with a view to defend his country and its laws; he puts not off the citizen when he enters the camp; but it is because he is a citizen, and would wish to continue so, that he makes for a while a soldier."[25] The echo of Machiavelli almost three centuries before—himself echoing early Greeks and Romans—is remarkable.

Not unexpectedly, the views of America's father were sought during the constitutional debate by a special committee appointed by Congress and chaired by Alexander Hamilton. In his "Sentiments on a Peace Establishment," George Washington responded in 1783 by suggesting four necessities. A small regular army was needed to protect against British or Spanish attacks, man seacoast and naval fortifications, and "awe the Indians." He also proposed the development of arsenals and weapons manufacturing capabilities. He advocated military academies to teach military sciences. Most important, because the standing army would be small (2,631, to be exact), Washington proposed a "respectable and well established Militia" which would be under national control and have uniform training and organizational standards. This centralized militia would be further supplemented by state militia patterned after the Continental militia, or Minutemen. In effect, Washington proposed a three-tiered land force: a regular army, a ready reserve similar to the volunteer militia, and an improved common militia.[26] Here we have the roots of "tiered readiness," the central premise of a new military structure (discussed more fully in chapter 6). Washington's recommendations reflected a pragmatic political judgment. He personally preferred a larger standing army but was aware of the resurgence of the prerevolutionary fear of a permanent army and knew it would be unacceptable.[27]

Not surprisingly, the leading Federalist supporter of a substantial standing army was Alexander Hamilton. His arguments, principally contained in *Federalist Papers* nos. 24, 25, 26, and 28, were founded much more strongly on the need to protect America's anticipated far-flung international commercial interests than to defend her borders from acquisitive European powers. "If we mean to be a commercial people," he wrote, "or even to be secure on our Atlantic side, we must endeavor, as soon as possible, to have a navy. To this purpose there must be dockyards and arsenals; and for the defense of these, fortifications, and probably garrisons." It was a short step from assuming a far-flung interest in peaceful commerce to establishing a network of military bases and forces to defend them.[28]

Hamilton, for the eventual majority opinion, placed great stress on the proposed constitutional power of the legislature (Congress) to constrain and regulate standing armies, especially in times of peace. "To the powers proposed to be conferred upon the federal government, in respect to the creation and direction of the national force, I have met with but one specific objection, which . . . is that, proper provision has not been made against the existence of standing armies in time of peace."[29] Hamilton's response was simple, assertive, and dismissive: ". . . restraints upon the discretion of the legislature in respect to military establishments would be improper to be imposed, and if imposed, from the necessities of society, would be unlikely to be observed." The three principal dangers to the new nation's security were, he argued, British and Spanish colonies still in the New World, "savage tribes on the Western frontier, and improvements in the art of navigation" by the Spanish and British. Hamilton observed that before and since the Revolution it had been necessary to maintain small garrisons on the Western frontier: "These garrisons must either be furnished by occasional detachments from the militia, or by permanent corps in the pay of the [national] government." Anticipating an early arms race, he argued that the British and Spanish would only augment their forces as the nation grew in strength and, therefore, "we should find it expedient to increase our frontier garrisons in some ratio to the force by which our Western settlements might be annoyed."

The classic republican argument against standing armies had already been raised in state constitutional debates. North Carolina and Pennsylvania included this interdiction in their constitutions: "As standing armies in time of peace are dangerous to liberty, they ought not to be kept." The bills of rights of New Hampshire, Delaware, Massachusetts, and Maryland contained a clause to this effect: "Standing armies are dangerous to liberty, and ought not to be kept without the consent of the legislature."

Hamilton, underscoring this last phrase, used it as the centerpiece of his Federalist case by noting that the British, Spanish, and Indian nations' threat encircled the Union from Maine to Georgia and thus was a common threat requiring a common—that is, federal—response. The principle of legislative consent to a standing army derived historically from William of Orange's defeat of James II in the English Revolution of 1688. In response to the dangerous authority represented by the 30,000 troops kept under arms by James II, the resulting Bill of Rights required that the consent of Parliament be given to raising or maintaining a standing army in peacetime. Following this principle, Hamilton argued that the proposed constitutional provision requiring legislative approval was sufficient protection against military ambition: "The legislature of the United States will be *obliged* by this provision, once at least in every two years [the limit on military authorization], to deliberate upon the propriety of keeping a military force on foot; to come to a new resolution on the point; and to declare their sense of the matter by a formal vote in the face of their constituents. They are not *at liberty* to invest in the executive department permanent funds for the support of an army, if they were even incautious enough to be willing to repose in it so improper a confidence."[30] One is curious to know what response Hamilton might make, more than two centuries later, to a circumstance in which the nation is at peace, with no threat to its borders, yet has in excess of 1.5 million men and women permanently under arms, at an annual cost of more than $250 billion and *no* debate in the legislature over the necessity, propriety, or purpose of this establishment.

The Federalists acknowledged the central role played by civilian militias in the Revolutionary War who "by their valor . . . erected eternal monuments to their fame." But militias simply were inadequate to defend against regular, disciplined armies: "War, like most other things, is a science to be acquired and perfected by diligence, by perseverance, by time, and by practice."[31] There remained the thorny issue of control of the militias. Now happy to acknowledge a well-regulated militia as "the most natural defense of a free country," Hamilton wanted it controlled by national, not state, government as "the guardian of the national security." Cannily, he acknowledges the fear of standing armies in aid of his argument for federal control of militias: "If the federal government can command the aid of the militia in those emergencies which call for the military arm in support of the civil magistrate, it can the better dispense with the employment of a different kind of force," i.e., a standing army.[32] Hamilton wanted to have the argument both ways.

More than one military historian has taken time to comment on the depth and breadth of fear of standing armies throughout revolutionary America. The fear of standing forces—brought to America from England with the earliest settlers—looms large in the history of the militia. Behind it was the greater fear of arbitrary, highly centralized government that with a force armed to compel obedience to it became even more dangerous to liberty. Because of the dual state-federal control under which it functioned, the militia seemed to many Americans the best security against that which they feared.[33]

As reasonable and balanced as the Federalists' arguments might seem today, anti-Federalist passions were aroused more by Congress's power, under Article I, section 8, "to raise and support armies" than by any other federal power. For most anti-Federalists the curse of this provision was not in any way diminished by the two-year limit on military appropriations. They argued that Britain's Parliament was limited to annual military funding. And they argued correctly that nothing would keep Congress from continuing appropriations indefinitely. Indeed. The historian Bernard Bailyn says that there is simply no way to measure the volume and fervor of the anti-Federalists' denunciations of this provision. It revived for them both a general fear of military power and the specific danger of standing armies, "a peculiar and distinctive threat to liberty that had been formulated for all time, they believed, in England in the 1690s, and had been carried forward intact to the colonies."[34]

Not surprisingly, none was more passionate in volume or fervor in opposition to the permanent standing army of the Federalists than Patrick Henry. "A standing army we shall also have," he thundered sarcastically, "to execute the execrable commands of tyranny. . . . Some way or other we must be a great and mighty empire; we must have an army, and a navy, and a number of things. . . ."[35] "Brutus," the anonymous and collective voice of the anti-Federalists, raised similar arguments from Roman and English history. In Rome, he argued, "the liberties of the commonwealth was [sic] destroyed, and the constitution overturned, by an army led by Julius Caesar, who was appointed to the command by the constitutional authority of that commonwealth. He changed it from a free republic . . . into that of the most absolute despotism. A standing army effected this change, and a standing army supported it through a succession of ages, which are marked in the annals of history, with the most horrid cruelties, bloodshed, and carnage . . . that ever punished or disgraced human nature. . . . The same army, that in Britain, vindicated the liberties of that people from the encroachments of despotism of a tyrant king, assisted Cromwell, their General, in wresting from the people, that liberty they had so dearly earned."[36] The anti-Federalists simply believed that a standing army, once established, could not be controlled.[37]

The Federalist idea that a standing national army would be counterbalanced by state militias was given short shrift by anti-Federalist opponents. Patrick Henry argued that garrisons of federal forces throughout the Union would represent the country's strongholds, far outweighing militia strength: "Of what service would they be to you [against superior federal forces], when most probably you will not have a single musket in the State; for as arms are to be provided by the Congress, they may or may not furnish them." He cites the proposed militia provision in the Constitution: "To provide for organizing, arming, and disciplining the militia, and for governing such part of them as may be employed in the service of the United States, reserving to the States respectively, the appointment of the officers, and the authority of training the militia, according to the discipline prescribed by Congress" (Article I, section 8, clause 16). Anticipating a struggle that would carry over into the twenty-first century, Henry concluded: "If they [Congress] neglect or refuse to discipline [i.e., train] or arm our militia, they will be useless: the States can do neither, this power being exclusively given to Congress: The power [of the States] of appointing officers over men not disciplined or armed, is ridiculous. . . ."[38]

Henry had support from other strong anti-Federalists such as George Mason who did not hold the national government above guilefully neglecting and failing to arm the state militias so that the people, in time of national crisis, would cry out to the national government, "Give us a standing army!" This is precisely what present-day National Guard officials say the federal government has historically done—neglect the militia—in order to strengthen support for the standing military. The standing army was an "engine of arbitrary power, which has so often and so successfully been used for the subversion of freedom," argued Luther Martin. The "bane of Republican governments," was the pejorative invoked by Samuel Nasson: "By this have seven-eighths of the once free nations of the globe been brought into bondage." "If a regular army is admitted will not the militia be neglected and gradually dwindle into contempt? And where then are we to look for defense of our rights and liberties?" demanded Elbridge Gerry. "With respect to a standing army, I believe there was not a member in the Federal convention who did not feel indignation at such an institution," Edmund Randolph told the Virginia convention, apparently conveniently overlooking the dominant Federalist faction.[39]

At issue, of course, was more than a strictly military question. At issue were two different visions of the new America.

One was of a commercial and political power whose strong central government could make treaties, collect taxes, form capital through a national bank, and enforce its will through a standing army—in short, something that looked to anti-Federalists like an imperial, and therefore potentially corrupt, state power. The other vision, based upon classical theory, radical Whig ideology, and republican idealism, was of a new nation of yeomen farmers controlling their own destinies and capable, as citizen-soldiers, of protecting their individual and collective interests. The Federalists' hopes for commercial growth and international prestige were, to the anti-Federalists, only the lust of ambitious men for a "splendid empire" which, according to the patterns of history, would burden the people with taxes, conscription, and campaigns.[40]

In this debate, Thomas Jefferson's voice became an important one. Since "the supreme power is ever possessed by those who have arms in their hands and are disciplined to the use of them," Jefferson wrote in his *Summary View of the Rights of British America* (1774), the danger to liberty lay in the supremacy "of a veteran army making the civil subordinate to the military instead of subjecting the military to the civil powers." In a clear return to the English Country-versus-Court debate a century before, Jefferson here and thereafter became a powerful defender of the Country position. As expansion of the standing army began for the early 1790s Indian campaign, Jefferson deplored it: "Every rag of an Indian depredation will . . . serve as a ground to raise troops with those who think a standing army and a public debt necessary for the happiness of the United States and we shall never be permitted to get rid of either." In his first inaugural address, Jefferson counted among the principles forming "the bright constellation which has gone before us, and guided our steps through an age of revolution and reformation . . . a well-disciplined militia, our best reliance in peace, and for the first moments of war, till regulars may relieve them. . . ."[41] Quaintly to the modern age, Jefferson clearly saw defenses as exactly that, a military capable of repelling attack but not of attacking anyone else. Thus, he stands modern defense on its head—militia will stand off the invaders until the regulars arrive. He would be amazed, but not amused, by a debate that featured deployment of regulars abroad to be supported eventually by reservists—the precise opposite of his vision. According to the military historian Russell Weigley, Jefferson believed that a citizenry trained and organized in arms would enable the standing army to be abolished. A universal military obligation should be practiced, and the natural aristocracy of talent and virtue should serve as the officers of the armed citizens.[42]

The cause of the standing army in peacetime could not have been strengthened by the widespread knowledge that its principal proponent was Alexander Hamilton, who managed personally to embody all the Caesarian qualities so frightening, if not loathsome, to the republican idealists. Hamilton's ambition to increase the Republic's permanent military strength, and the widespread suspicion that he hoped to head that strength himself, confirmed his critics in their belief that rule by a strong executive, supported by the interests of concentrated wealth, would lead inevitably to rule by a standing army that would be both dictatorial and corrupt.[43]

To curb Hamiltonian-Federalist ambition, the anti-Federalists proposed their own amendment to the Constitution on June 27, 1788, only the first part of which was to survive in the form of the controversial Second Amendment later adopted:

> That the people have a right to keep and bear arms; that a well-regulated militia, composed of the body of the people trained to arms, is the proper, natural, and safe defense of a free state; that standing armies, in time of peace, are dangerous to liberty, and therefore ought to be avoided, as far as the circumstances and protection of the community will admit; and that, in all cases, the military should be under strict subordination to, and governed by, the civil power. [The Second Amendment reads: "A well regulated Militia, being necessary to the security of a free State, the right of the people to keep and bear Arms, shall not be infringed."][44]

Not unexpectedly, it fell to James Madison to negotiate resolution of the standing army dispute between Federalists and anti-Federalists, and he did so by coming down on the Federalist side but without raising the personal animosity and suspicion that Hamilton did.

Madison argued that the two greatest safeguards against unwarranted assumption of power by the military were the strength of the Union itself against internal conflict or insurrection and, second, the two-year limit on congressional appropriations for the military. Unity itself was the nation's greatest defense: "America united, with a handful of troops, or without a single soldier, exhibits a more forbidding posture to foreign ambition than America disunited, with a hundred thousand veterans ready for combat." Employing profound common sense, Madison thus deftly stood the broader anti-Federalist argument on its head.

In the context of a discussion in *The Federalist Papers* of the stability and autonomy of state governments under the shadow of what many considered to be an oppressive national government, Madison addressed the "visionary supposition" that the federal government would accumulate a military force either to repress the states or to undertake foreign expeditions. Assume, he wrote, using Jeffersonian mathematical logic, that the national government formed the largest army it could from the postrevolutionary population of approximately 3 million people. Standard calculations of the day held that the maximum permanent force any nation's population and resources could support was one one-hundredth of the entire population or one twenty-fifth part of all those (men) able to bear arms. This, he calculated, would yield a federal army no larger than 25,000 to 30,000 men under arms. "The State governments with the people on their side," he argued, "would be able to repel the danger," for, against the federal forces "would be opposed a militia amounting to near half a million citizens with arms in their hands."[45] Thus, Madison assumed full-strength local militias made up of one in six of all American citizens. (Using this same calculation today, the United States would have citizen militias numbering more than 40 million, and, following Madison, that would presumably include only men, not women.)

Needless to say, the Madisonian-Hamiltonian view prevailed and a standing army we did have, to the great dismay of Patrick Henry and the anti-Federalists. One central feature of the Federalists' post-Constitution military policy was to create a centrally controlled, uniform militia system. As always, fearing a "federal take-over" of state and local militias, the anti-Federalists successfully blocked this effort. It was a triumph of ideology over military requirements, for state militias ever since have regularly been less well trained and equipped than they would have been under a more uniform national militia system. The states thus traded efficiency for autonomy. The legislative result of this standoff was an innocuous and ineffective Uniform Militia Act passed in 1792, during Washington's first administration; it provided no funds, coordinated system, or enforcement provisions, and therefore was quickly disregarded.

The anti-Federalist, republican cause would shortly find support in the conversion of the French revolutionary army of citizens into a Napoleonic army of Continental conquest of well over 1 million more or less professional soldiers. The Grande Armée had become, in the Clausewitzian sense, "an instrument of state power rather than of ideology."[46] Between 1803 and 1815, Bonaparte led this army first against the Hapsburg territories in Italy, then against Austria, Prussia, Spain, and Russia. Based upon his study of Napoleonic use of power, Clausewitz formulated his theories of war as a political act carried out by one state against another. This institutionalization of military power as an instrument of statecraft was precisely what American republicans and anti-Federalists feared and opposed.

Under Jefferson's early-nineenth-century presidency, states'-rights' military hopes finally died. Even as he continued to support the militia ideal, Jefferson had finally accepted the necessity for a regular army before he became president. His compromise was to "republicanize" the Army by purging the officer corps of Federalists and establishing the U.S. Military Academy to educate officers committed to republican values.[47] Thereafter, in 1815, Madison's efforts to develop professional and permanent government institutions in Washington included the military, and any hope for a retreat to citizen armies controlled at the local level disappeared.

Within a few years, the great French observer, Alexis de Tocqueville, arrived to assess what the Americans had wrought. He brought with him what might be called a pragmatic-republican prism through which he viewed life in the new Union and the military role as part of it. ". . . a large army amongst a democratic people will always be a great danger; the most effectual means of diminishing that danger would be to reduce the army, but this is a remedy which all nations are not able to apply," he wrote. But then he took note of America's strongest defense, geography: "Fortune, which has conferred so many peculiar benefits upon the inhabitants of the United States, has placed them in the middle of a wilderness, where they have, so to speak, no neighbors; a few thousand soldiers are sufficient for their wants; but this is peculiar to America, not democracy."[48]

Some of this "island nation" outlook was shared by President Thomas Jefferson when, in 1801, his first year in office, he undertook to reduce the young U.S. Navy substantially. Following the Naval Peace Establishment Act, signed in the closing hours of the John Adams presidency, and under pressure from his fiscally austere treasury secretary, Albert Gallatin, Jefferson disposed of most of the navy's capital ships except, as the act directed, for thirteen frigates, only six of which were kept in active service. Four years later, however, at the beginning of his second term, Jefferson authorized a program of gunboat construction to enhance the coastal defenses. Almost a century later, Alfred Thayer Mahan argued that, except for Jefferson's "abhorrence of navies," "we probably should have had no war of 1812." Acknowledging that Jefferson was, in the main, carrying out Adams' own policy, Adams himself stated that Jefferson was more a navy man than either Washington or Hamilton, or even his successor, James Madison.

Tocqueville evidenced more interest in the sociology of democratic armies, however, than in their size and practical functions. He observed that the equality of conditions characterizing democracies did not exempt them from the need for armies and those armies "always exercise a powerful influence over their fate." He particularly noted the difference between "aristocratic armies" in which the officers exercise a conservative and therefore restraining influence because they alone "have retained a strict connection with civil society and never forego their purpose of resuming their place in it sooner or later," and "democratic armies" in which private soldiers on the other hand "stand in this position, and from the same cause."[49] He believed strongly that recruits in democratic armies mirrored the qualities and values of the communities from which they came: "If that community is enlightened and energetic, the community itself will keep them within the bounds of order." Tocqueville saw a direct relation between civil and military principles. "Teach the citizens to be educated, orderly, firm, and free and the soldiers will be disciplined and obedient."[50] Thus, he believed, "The remedy for the vices of the army is not to be found in the army itself, but in the country."[51]

Matters become more complicated for democracies, according to Tocqueville, when they move from structuring their forces to actual war fighting. "If democratic nations are naturally prone to peace from their interests and propensities, they are constantly drawn to war and revolutions by their armies." Tocqueville believed that war developed in otherwise peaceful men the propensity for violence and despotism: "All those who seek to destroy the liberties of a democratic nation ought to know that war is the shortest and surest means to accomplish it. This is the first axiom of the science."[52] So, he is caught in the paradox of armed democracies. They require at least some military institutions—a standing army and the means to equip it—for their defense and security. If the soldiers for this force are drawn from a stable, well-ordered, and educated civil society, they will reflect these values. But the more professional and institutionalized these military forces are, the more inclined they are toward conflict that educates these soldiers in the codes of despotism and violence and undermines the very democracies they are meant to secure. For this conundrum Tocqueville could find no resolution, except in this aphorism: "There are two things that a democratic people will find most difficult, to begin a war and to end it."

For the twenty-five hundred or more years leading up to the founding of the United States, virtually any consideration of republican forms of government involved, sooner or later, serious debate over the role of the military. More often than not, this debate was central to the nature of the republic. The instinctive and informed belief of political thinkers over time, repeatedly confirmed by experience that began with the Romans, was of a direct correlation between standing armies and imperial aspiration. Rarely did a nation at peace require a professional army except to further its ambitions for political power, commercial advantage, or both, abroad. For the theorists of the republican ideal, standing armies inevitably became symbols of political corruption, commercial enterprise, centralized authority, concentrated wealth, power, influence, prerogative, and the Court over the Country.

Confronted, as they believed, by persistent British and Spanish colonial ambitions in the New World, as well as by Native American hostility, real and imagined, on the frontier, moderate Federalists of the Madisonian persuasion prevailed in the Federalist–anti-Federalist debate and convinced a majority of their colleagues to authorize a modest standing army, with the proviso that Congress could authorize expenditures for it no further than two years into the future. This spending limitation, together with overwhelming numbers of the citizenry armed and at large, were believed to be sufficient to counterbalance unwarranted military ambition.

Along with many other perpetually perplexing paradoxes left unresolved in the constitutional debate, the legal and political relationships between the standing federal army, created by Article I, section 8, clause 12 of the Constitution, and the state militia, authorized in clause 16 of the same section, were largely left for time and experience to work out. For 220 years, this paradoxical relationship has had a rough and uneasy life persisting to this day. An understanding of this complex association, something akin to jealous lovers or quarrelsome siblings, is necessary to an appreciation of the U.S. military situation in the post–Cold War era. For the second half of the twentieth century, America *was* Roosevelt's "great arsenal of democracy." Before and during that period, the battle going on *inside* the arsenal often gave off as much heat, if not bloodshed, as the battles outside.

Of the historic contest between regulars and reserves, standing army and citizen militia, in America, it would not be inappropriate to quote Wellington at Waterloo: "Hard pounding this, gentlemen; let's see who will pound longest."

Chapter 5

Why Do We Have Two Armies?

... a fight between two bald men over a comb.
Jorge Luis Borges, on the Falklands War

For the unconcerned civilian, the two-century struggle between the regulars and the reserve, the permanent Army and the National Guard, bears all the excitement of a schoolboy scuffle. Boys and their toys. Except the boys are men, many with long military careers, and the toys are real guns, some of which can fire a great distance and kill a great number of people. The contest, largely conducted out of public view, has been a fierce one, and unlike academic politics, the stakes have been—and are—quite high.

It is not accidental that the two American armies existed with minimum friction until the nation began its complex transition from an inward-looking, frontier-seeking, insular, agrarian society to an outward-looking, muscle-flexing, industrial world power. Nor is it coincidental that the polarization between the two armies produced polar-opposite intellectual champions on each side. As the United States launched an oceangoing fleet designed to protect and promote its increasing stature as a global trader and empire builder, its military professionals increasingly felt the need to separate themselves from the image of rustic frontier minutemen and parochial state militiamen and to establish their credentials as serious military competitors of their European counterparts. But, as the federal army expanded in power and influence, prophets of the republican ideal would emerge to remind the nation of its populist military heritage. No more dramatic way can be found to illustrate the widening chasm between the army of the Court of Washington, the army of central federal power and Rooseveltian (Theodore) nationalism on the one hand, and the army of the Country of America, the army of the people and the local community on the other, than through the lives, writings, and philosophy of two military intellectuals, Emory Upton and John McAuley Palmer.

A Regular Army officer, Emory Upton wrote *The Military Policy of the United States,* which was for many years the definitive work on U.S. military matters.[1] Upton stressed the central role played by America's standing army and the very peripheral and collateral role of state militias. Indeed, he went out of his way to anticipate the "calamities, confusion, and chaos" attendant on the use of citizen-soldiers in the Spanish-American War and in early-twentieth-century skirmishes on the Mexican border. The Uptonian view of military history stressed the importance of a fully professional army in support of national aspirations, the mischievous effects of civilian control over the military, and the great dangers attendant upon reliance on state-controlled militias which, in his view, were inadequate, amateurish, poorly trained, and ill-equipped.

Upton's importance, on the eve of a century of world wars hot and cold, was to shape private and public debate in favor of the permanent professional over the citizen-soldier.

Upton's unchallenged influence is difficult to overestimate. As essentially the first historian of the U.S. Army and a potent partisan of the standing-army school, he dominated American military thought until the emergence of his rival and philosophical counterpart, John McAuley Palmer. According to Russell Weigley, Upton was a Regular Army professional "bitterly contemptuous" of citizen-soldiers. Even though Weigley finds him contemptuous also of many American social values, his work stood alone and had such great influence for so long that his views influenced almost everything written about American military history. Military historians who continue to write disparagingly of the "myth of the militia" borrow this phrase from Emory Upton.[2]

Forces were at work, however, to counter the Uptonian professionalist-nationalist view. Following the Civil War, state militiamen were painfully aware of becoming increasingly entrenched in their second-class military status and totally dependent on the Regular Army for equipment and training, neither of which was readily or regularly forthcoming. In 1879, these citizen-soldiers organized a lobby in the form of a National Guard Association to seek recognition and identity. The phrase "National Guard," used to describe the disparate citizen militias in the post–American revolutionary period, originated with the young French volunteer general the Marquis de Lafayette, who used the phrase *Garde Nationale* during the French Revolution to mean any citizen militia and who applied the same term to all organized militias during his 1824 return to the United States.[3] Through the efforts of the National Guard lobby, a new Militia Act (1903) replaced the ineffective 1792 law and recognized "the Guard as the first line reserve," extending "federal aid to state military forces," and imposing "a degree of federal control on the National Guard."[4]

The National Guard sought recognition and support from the national government while seeking to preserve its autonomy under state control. It wished to maintain control of its organization and officer selection system while continuing to be the principal source of manpower in time of national conflict. This hope was dashed by two developments in quick succession: first, passage of the National Defense Act (1916), which gave the federal government much greater jurisdiction over state militias, their officer selection systems, and their assignment to regular army units; and, second, the adoption of a selective service system during the World War I mobilization effort in 1917, which effectively ended the traditional reliance by the national government on the states for manpower recruitment.

The second National Defense Act (1920) sought to bring some rationality to the dual federal-state military system by recognizing both Regular Army and National Guard divisions. But, perhaps further to marginalize state military forces, Congress created yet another military layer in the form of the Organized Reserve. The Organized Reserve was meant to be, at least in part, a source of trained manpower mobilization apart from and not under the control of the states.

This action reflected another debate tracing to the nineenth century regarding the regular-reserve relationship. The issue was whether to create a national reserve under federal control or to continue to rely on the state-controlled National Guard as the principal support and source of manpower for the standing Army. Not surprisingly, the Regular Army preferred the creation of a pure national reserve under control of the national government. Those who believed in maintaining the National Guard as the principal reserve force could not agree on its authority, role, or mission. Some supported a local National Guard mission of defending national fortifications against attack. Guardsmen from inland states, however, not fearing invasion, sought a more aggressive role as the principal organized elements for assignment to combat overseas. The Guard's lack of unity regarding purpose and mission would continue to plague supporters of the concept of citizen-soldiers as the mainstream reserves.[5]

The constitutional paradox (enshrined in Article I, section 8) continues to perplex military and civilian commanders and policy makers throughout the twentieth century. The crux of the struggle concerned these issues: Will the authority to mobilize manpower rest with the federal or state governments? Will the principal reserve units be National Guard (state) or Organized Reserve (federal)? What is the federal responsibility, represented by the Regular Army, for equipping, training, and preparing National Guard units? Once mobilized, will National Guard units serve under their own, citizen officers or under Regular Army officers? In combat, how will Regular Army and National Guard units be operationally integrated? In combat, will Guard personnel fill individual slots or serve in the units with which they have trained?

Two late-nineteenth- and early-twentieth-century developments further complicated these already thorny questions.

First, widespread industrial unrest brought on by efforts to organize industrial workers led to National Guard units in a number of states being called up to deal with civil disorder and labor strife. Consequently, National Guardsmen were labeled strikebreakers. Between 1877 and 1903 state governors called out the Guard more than seven hundred times, and about half of the calls were for the Guard to perform strike police duty. Since many working people viewed the Guard as a capitalist tool and disliked it intensely, strike police duty was onerous for Guardsmen who would, as often as not, come from the local community torn by the strife.[6] This period of mining and industrial strife during the 1880s and '90s was a dismal one for the Guard. It had no foreign enemies against which to defend. Therefore, a new Guard recruit could find duty only on "the raw, rough, unexplored, bloody industrial frontier within his own State." In the North, the National Guard became the balance of power between capital and labor. These domestic labor wars adversely affected the growth, military horizons, and training of both the National Guard and the Regular Army. The Guard was placed on the defensive for being willing to serve its state and national governments in these nasty domestic crises. Its reputation suffered for decades thereafter.[7]

Second, the rise of the Progressive reform movement during the late nineteenth and early twentieth centuries led to an expanded regulatory role for the national government in response to the rising power of large industrial corporations and to adverse public reaction to abuses arising from this corporate concentration. The Progressive reliance on central regulatory policies carried over into military affairs, where the emphasis was on professionalism, nationalism, and centralized authority, all of which operated against a local, irregular, citizen-based militia system.

The issue was tested at the end of the century during the Spanish-American War, when President McKinley surprised the Regular Army by mobilizing 125,000 Guardsmen, more than twice what the War Department thought necessary and approximately the limit of Guard strength. "Calling out fewer would alienate those Guardsmen unable to volunteer, dampening martial enthusiasm and courting political disaster," McKinley said. Besides, he wanted to avoid a perceived mistake by Lincoln decades earlier in failing to mobilize sufficient reserve forces at the outset of the Civil War. McKinley had in mind to intimidate Spain with a national show of force.[8]

Into this potent mix of arguments arrived a career military officer, John McAuley Palmer, who came to represent the citizen-soldier counterbalance to Emory Upton. Referring to the two-decade, between-war years from 1919 and 1939, no less an authority than General George Marshall called Palmer "the Army's leading intellectual." Though a West Point graduate and Regular Army officer, Palmer came by his republican military philosophy honestly. His grandfather had commanded the XIV Corps of the Army of the Cumberland in the Civil War. The elder Palmer had come out of that war as a volunteer officer with a strong resentment of the Regular Army and what he called "the West Point crowd." He had resigned his commission in a promotional dispute with William Tecumseh Sherman, but President Lincoln refused his resignation and made Palmer military governor of Kentucky. His dispute with Sherman was largely over the belief held by Sherman, General Winfield Scott, and others that military leadership should rest in a monopoly held by professional officers. The elder Palmer joined Generals Ulysses S. Grant, George H. Thomas, and others in believing that military leadership, no less than political and economic leadership, in a republic should be open to Jefferson's natural aristocracy—able civilians with innate leadership qualities.

Preparing for his departure for West Point in 1898, the young Palmer sought the advice of his eighty-five-year-old grandfather, then a U.S. senator from Illinois. Responding to the young man's argument for a larger Regular Army, the old veteran said: "If that's what you want, John McAuley, why don't you organize and train a citizen army in time of peace? That will cost less money and will give you many more soldiers ready for defense. Your 50,000 extra regulars won't help much in a big war unless you have a citizen army to put behind them. And if you have a citizen army to put behind them, you won't need 50,000 extra regulars."[9]

The elder Palmer instilled in his grandson the strong belief that professionalization of the officer class would produce a highly privileged militarist or samurai caste that would be inconsistent with the genius of democratic institutions. He further urged that his grandson not let West Point make him a narrow Regular Army partisan, reminding him that George Washington, Nathaniel Greene, and all other American Continental Army officers were citizen-soldiers. He might also have observed that many of these same officers would later found the Order of the Cincinnatus to celebrate the agrarian-populist citizen-consul of the early Roman republic. Later the young Palmer would discover that Washington, the American Cincinnatus, had first proposed military academies not to create a professional officer corps but to provide technical in-struction for future citizen-officers.

A brigade commander in France during World War I, Palmer came away from that experience with two important lessons. First, he shared with Marshal Foch a belief that re-serve officers of broad cultivation and wide-ranging outlook and experience may be preferable to a better-trained regular officer more narrowly interested in petty military politics or preoccupied with promotion. He also learned the vital lesson of unit cohesion. His responsibility for manpower distribution gave him an understanding of how intensively men disliked being uprooted from the units to which they were accus-tomed. Officers who were frequently moved from one com-pany or battalion to another found it difficult to create cohesion with their new commands. When dealing with their own troops made up of fellow Guardsmen from their own town, they excelled. But when they were required to com-mand a group of strangers, the adjustment was almost always distressing. Men returning from hospital recuperation who were assigned to units other than their own found the adjust-ment most painful.[10] Despite this experience and the clear ev-idence of human nature, the policy of the regular U.S. military is, to this day, to rotate individual soldiers frequently from unit to unit, making unit cohesion virtually impossible.

Following World War I, and pursuing his effort to apply military theories rooted in history to the nation's postwar defenses, Palmer researched the original intent of the first commander-in-chief. While exploring George Washington's papers, in an attempt to establish that both Abraham Lincoln in the Civil War and Woodrow Wilson in World War I had failed to heed Washington's advice to rely primarily on citizen-soldiers, he discovered hitherto unknown manuscripts in the Library of Congress. In 1783 (as noted above) when the revolutionary army was disbanding, Congress requested Washington's views on the nature of its peacetime military establishment. In conventional military fashion, Washington requested opinions from his senior subordinates, Generals Knox, Lincoln, Pickering, and von Steuben. In his report to Congress, Washington relied most heavily on von Steuben, who advocated a Swiss system of citizen-soldiers as most appropriate for democracies.[11]

Largely as a result of this discovery, Palmer became a life-long advocate of the Swiss model, devoting much of his book *Statesmanship or War*[12] to explication of this system as it might apply to the United States. His intellectual contribution covers the quarter-century between the end of World War I through the close of World War II, and consistently stresses the need for America to rely on an army of the people. Palmer was largely responsible for drafting the National Defense Act (1920) which specifically institutionalized National Guard divisions parallel to their Regular Army counterparts. He confronted, but could not resolve, the dilemma embodied in the Constitution. Although the 1920 act placed control of the civilian or Guard units under the states, pursuant to the so-called "militia provision" of the Constitution (Article I, section 8, clause 16), Palmer believed that the Guard, like the Organized Reserve, should be formed under the "army clause" (Article I, section 8, clause 12), thus making the citizen-soldiers a more direct and vital part of the national defense forces.

But for him, the central question was less whether federal or state governments should control the citizen militia and more whether the majority of the national defense force should be well-trained citizens rather than standing army professionals. The central theme of Palmer's thought was keeping the military establishment democratic, or as he expressed it, of devising a system of defense suited to the genius of a democratic people. General George Marshall sensed this core value when he called Palmer the "civilian conscience of the Army." Even as a Regular Army officer and West Point graduate, Palmer promoted the role of the citizen-soldier throughout his life out of a belief that a strong civilian component in the military establishment was the surest safeguard against the abuse of military power.[13]

The threat of military adventurism could best be forestalled, Palmer believed, by incorporating citizen-soldiers throughout the military establishment, from privates up through the highest levels of command. A citizen army was essentially defensive in nature, and would more effectively resist the temptation toward acquisitive conflict or imperial conquest than would a permanent standing military. Palmer also believed that, by integrating a people's army more closely into the nation's foreign policy, citizens would be more involved in the debate concerning their country's objectives abroad. The Regular Army should be kept small, he said, while the organized units of citizen-soldiers in political jurisdictions across the country who formed the bulk of the nation's defenses would ensure against a dangerous centralization of power, the misuse of military might, and violation of the nation's democratic principles. In section 5 of the 1920 National Defense

Act, he devised a scheme of committees for the administration of the reserves and citizen militias, having a mixed membership of civilians and military careerists, both as a means of providing further opportunities for senior command to the most qualified citizen-soldiers and of integrating reserve and regular units. Palmer insisted on the distinction between universal military *training,* which he favored to ensure the preparedness of citizen forces, and universal military *service,* or conscription, which enabled a commander-in-chief to commit forces with or without congressional review and approval.

Perhaps more than any other twentieth-century officer, John McAuley Palmer saw the nation's military as an integral part of a democratic society. His studies of history, military theory, and the nature of democratic government led him to conclude that a nation that wished to remain free must create military institutions consistent with the genius of a democratic people and must find the *balance* between liberty and security required to prevent the military establishment from dominating the nation.[14]

Fifty years later, Palmer remains worthy of extended attention. He was not only the Army's conscience but also its leading intellectual. He gave more serious thought and attention than any of his contemporaries to the relationship of military establishments to democratic republics, and he anticipated trends that would haunt the military establishment of the second half of the century. "He understood," writes his biographer I. B. Holley, "as many of his younger contemporaries did not, that the manpower of the nation should never be mobilized without first mobilizing the national will. The humiliating disaster in Vietnam stands as compelling evidence of the national failure to grasp this insight which suffused Palmer's thinking."[15]

In the post–Cold War years, Palmer's application of the Swiss military model to the United States deserves consideration. In 1914, the Swiss mobilized a modern, organized army of 300,000 men in four days from a total population of 4 million at a cost of only $27 per soldier. The Swiss trained 1 soldier for every 13 citizens in the post–World War I years, while the United States would have to train only 1 in 230 citizens to mobilize an army of a half-million during the same period. This ratio could be satisfied and the Swiss model adopted if only 1 young American in every 17 would *voluntarily* undertake the same training and service that every young Swiss man is *required* to undertake. Under the Swiss system, an infantryman underwent 65 days of recruit training, followed by 11 days of drills for each of the next seven summers. Thus, for a lifetime 28-year obligation (from age 18 to 45), each Swiss male gave his country 153 days, or less than 6 days per year.

For Palmer, the democratization of the Swiss officer corps and the correlation between military leadership and democratic citizenship were of utmost importance. He noted that all Swiss male citizens were required to be trained for service in the national defense army, but that any Swiss private could rise to the highest command provided he prepared himself for each step in promotion and meet the standard tests of capacity for leadership. "Switzerland draws her military leaders as she draws her political and industrial leaders," he said, "from all of the people and not from a small and highly privileged class." Palmer further believed that leaders of the Swiss army also became the leaders of Swiss democracy: "Their training for national defense is the foundation of their training for democratic citizenship."[16]

In this connection, Palmer drew a sharp contrast with both German aristocracy and the American North in pre–Civil War days. Referring to Bismarck's military outlook, Palmer said, "The [German] army was officered by its aristocracy and was maintained as a school for drilling the German masses in subservience to aristocracy"; ". . . universal training in Switzerland was designed to develop democratic leadership; in Germany it was designed to destroy it."[17] Referring to the Civil War period, Palmer argued that people will sacrifice their lives for a cause only if they are spiritually prepared to die for their convictions—that is to say, if the cause engages their convictions. Separation of citizenship from military service caused most American politicians, especially in the North prior to the Civil War, to be ignorant of military service as a positive civic virtue.

Reversing current practice, Palmer (like Washington) believed that the standing army should undertake no mission that could be effectively performed by the citizen army.[18] Money spent in violation of this principle would unduly inflate the defense budget and actually impair the strength and efficiency of the nation's defenses. Palmer argued further that the technical experts required for national defense were already 90 percent trained by private industries and should be maintained as citizen-soldiers at industry expense rather than as costly, professional military personnel maintained at taxpayers' expense.[19] Under Palmer's militia system, the citizen army would have principal responsibility for continental (home) defense, and the regular or professional army and navy elements would provide forces for foreign garrisoning, on the rare occasions needed, and for continued training and readiness of citizen defenses.

Unnecessary reliance on foreign resources and a large professional army to help procure them was, for Palmer, nothing short of scandalous. Eerily anticipating America's dependence on Mideast oil in the late twentieth century, Palmer wrote: "It is America's most valuable military asset that her capacity for self-subsistence is great. It would, therefore, be absurd for her to develop foreign commerce to the extent of sacrificing this great strategic advantage. For her to make herself dependent upon naval power as a consequence of neglecting her capacity for self-subsistence would be an unspeakable folly."[20] As an island nation with vast raw material reserves, America could construct an impregnable defense using citizen-soldiers without showing a provocative face to its trading partners.

Put simply, reliance on professional military institutions for national security was for Palmer a provocation and a sign of weakness rather than of security and strength. He steadfastly resisted the notion, so popular today, that weapons had become too sophisticated for use by other than professionals and that war was too complex for citizen-soldiers. New weapons should immediately be made available to citizen-soldiers and not be used as pretexts for justifying expansion of the professionals' exclusive prerogatives, Palmer thought. America had, by the invention of the modern federal system, shown the world how to reconcile national union and local self-government. "But by the invention of the modern army of the people, Switzerland shows us how to make democracy immortal."[21]

Palmer's great legacy to a twenty-first-century national defense philosophy is simply this: *"A free state cannot continue to be democratic in peace and autocratic in war. Standing armies threaten government by the people, not because they consciously seek to pervert liberty, but because they relieve the people themselves of the duty of self-defense. A people accustomed to let a special class defend them must sooner or later become unfit for liberty."* An army *of* the people must be among the vital institutions of a government *by* the people. Palmer believed that the maintenance of a single professional soldier more than necessary threatened the very groundwork of free institutions.[22]

Perhaps the high-water mark for Palmer's doctrine was represented by War Department Circular No. 347, issued by then U. S. Army Chief of Staff George Marshall on August 25, 1944, as doctrine for the post-World War II military. Therein, Marshall proposed

> a professional peace establishment (no larger than necessary to meet normal peacetime requirements) to be reinforced in time of emergency by organized units drawn from a citizen army reserve, effectively organized for this purpose in time of peace, with full opportunity for competent citizen soldiers to acquire practical experience through temporary active service and to rise by successive steps to any rank for which they can be definitely qualified; and with specific facilities for such practical experience, qualification, and advancement definitely organized as essential and predominating characteristics of the peace establishment.[23]

Shortly thereafter, General Dwight D. Eisenhower replaced Marshall as army chief of staff and rescinded Circular No. 347, even though, ironically, as president almost fifteen years later Eisenhower was to issue his famous warning against a "military-industrial complex."

Several military historians and scholars have observed the strong continuity of thought running from Palmer's 1912 report on U.S. land forces through his contribution to the watershed National Defense Act of 1920, and even into the planning of U.S. participation in World War II. In the end, few can doubt that Palmer's impact on American military philosophy has far exceeded that of his archrival, Emory Upton.[24] Their respective careers and philosophies deserve serious consideration, because together they vividly represent the bookends of modern American military thought. The intellectual framework provided by Palmer as embodied in the 1920 National Defense Act and George Marshall's support for Palmer's concept of an army of the people set the intellectual high-water mark for the concept of national defense based upon the citizen-soldier.

Even today, many military professionals persist in the belief that the Guard is ill trained, ill equipped, and unprepared for a combat role. The Guard's traditional response is that responsibility for training, equipping, preparing, and integrating the Guard into combat units rests with the Regular Army which, it strongly suspects, is concerned that the Guard would prove too effective in combat and would undermine the doctrine that only a regular, standing force can succeed in the modern battlefield.

The regular-versus-reserve struggle today focuses more often than not on the single, all-purpose word "readiness." It is not a word without content in professional circles. There are normally five categories used to measure readiness: personnel strength, individual skill qualification, equipment level, equipment condition, and unit training. Each of the five categories is measured under a grading system called SORTS (Status of Resources and Training System) by levels ranging from 90 percent or better to below 60 or 70 percent. However, scores in each of these categories, especially nonquantifiables such as individual skills, are bound to be more subjective than scientific. Further, even the most dedicated social scientist has yet to find an accurate measure of such great human intangibles as motivation, morale, and esprit de corps.[25]

In one category especially, that of effective training time, a sharp distinction must be drawn between the "business as usual" of current military practice and the massively reformed system advocated here. Few would deny that reserve units have not been effectively equipped and trained in the past. There has often been a wide gap between "available" and "effective" training time for reservists, that is, the difference between the total time required of a reservist and the time actually dedicated to military training. Misuse of reservists' time under traditional conditions of reserve training is the product of a system dedicated to considering the reserves as second-class military citizens.

A review of regular-reserve relations reveals a constant pattern. When the Guard is called up, it is routinely found deficient as a viable ready reserve in critical categories such as training, officer education, equipment, or coordination between the upper echelons of command and the maneuver units in regiments, brigades, and divisions. Equally important, the Regular Army has lacked workable mobilization plans, violated Guard unit integrity despite premobilization policies, drawn experienced Guard officers and noncommissioned officers for other assignments, and used Guardsmen as fillers for under-strength regular units. From the Guard perspective, the most striking aspect of the relationship is the Regular Army's persistent indifference and hostility toward the Guard.

The National Guard's history and tradition have not made its relations with the Regular Army easier. Even though originally formed as *local* militias under state control (pursuant to Article I, section 8, clause 16 of the Constitution), the National Guard Association has lobbied vigorously for a greater role in *national* military matters and, in the twentieth century, greater support from the Regular Army. Some elements of the National Guard at some periods have seemed to want it both ways—to preserve its autonomy as a state creature with independent constitutional status on the one hand and to make the Guard an integral, vital part of the national defense forces on the other.

During early-twentieth-century military reform, Congress recognized an organized militia in the form of the National Guard and an unorganized militia represented by able-bodied men obligated to both national and state service in times of emergency. In exchange for increased federal funding, arms, and equipment, the Organized Militia, or National Guard, was to meet federal standards for commissioning officers, recruitment of enlisted men, field training, and paralleling Army regular unit organization. The Militia Act (1908) removed restrictions on Guard units serving overseas and time limits on call-ups in exchange for permission to deploy the Guard as units rather than individual replacements. This legislation also established the National Guard Bureau in the War Department, which was designed to be the channel of communications between the federal and state governments, but which became, itself, a creature of the federal military.[26] (Through the office of the attorney general, the Army's judge advocate general later ruled the provision for compulsory overseas service by Guardsmen to be unconstitutional.)

As the U.S. looked toward the possibility of becoming involved in World War I, the National Defense Act (1916) provided that the primary reserve force would be the National Guard whose members would be required to take a dual federal-state oath upon enlistment: "Guardsmen could be compelled to serve abroad for unlimited periods of time in a national emergency, but they would go to war as Guard units, not as individuals."[27] The War Department was to screen Guard officers and establish physical and mental standards for Guard recruits. From the reservists' point of view, the most significant aspects of the 1916 Defense Act were the provision to utilize state militias for national defense purposes—this against a sweeping effort to reduce the Guard to a local constabulary role—and the provisions that prepared the way for a new national draft law.[28]

Still frustrated by the original constitutional paradox, Congress made yet another effort at structuring regular-reserve national defenses with the National Defense Act of 1920. It provided for a multitiered system based on voluntary participation and diverse degrees or "tiers" of readiness.[29] There was to be a regular army of 280,000, supplemented by a National Guard which could reach levels of 435,000 in peacetime, and an organized federal reserve force, composed initially of World War I veterans, responsible for maintaining "skeleton division" headquarters. Based upon this tiered system, planners from the General Staff estimated that a sixty-day intense mobilization period would produce an army of 2.3 million men. One of the most important aspects of the 1920 act was the creation of a system for commissioning reserve officers through the new Reserve Officers Training Corps, which produced 80,000 reserve officers for active duty upon U.S. mobilization in 1940.[30] Once again facing determined opposition from Regular Army advocates and Uptonian military theorists, the National Guard received a ringing endorsement from a singular hero of the Great War, General John J. Pershing: "The National Guard never received the whole-hearted support of the Regular Army during the [First] World War. There was always more or less prejudice against them, and our Regular Army officers failed to perform their full duty as component instructors, and often criticized when they should have instructed. The National Guard people resented this and properly so."[31] During World War I, eighteen National Guard divisions and seventeen nondivisional regiments served in Europe. (Defeated German military units reported that National Guard divisions were the best and the toughest they faced in World War I.) Based on their performance as characterized by leaders such as Pershing, the 1920 act laid the basis for the role the National Guard plays today. It rejected efforts by the Uptonians to create a purely professional standing army dominated by career officers with little if any combat role for citizen-soldiers in time of conflict or national emergency.

Matters became even more complex with the formation of the Army Reserve in 1920 and the creation (by a 1933 amendment to the 1920 act) of a National Guard governed not by the "militia clause" of the Constitution but by the "army clause." The Regular Army has shown during most periods the same disdain for the Army Reserve that it has for the National Guard. But, like the National Guard, the Army Reserve mounted its own successful lobby and was able to block a 1966–67 Defense Department effort to merge it with the Guard."

The tidal pull of the Upton-Palmer struggle continues to dominate the second half of the century. The Cold War years were characterized by a permanent standing army composed of professionals and conscripts. The National Guard was used by President Truman in Korea largely "to restore the strategic reserve in the U.S."[32] and virtually not at all by President Johnson in Vietnam. In large part, Johnson feared testing the strength of popular opinion at the local level in support of American involvement in Vietnam. He refused to mobilize reserve components despite several recommendations from the Joint Chiefs of Staff to do so, apparently fearing that a reserve call-up would provoke public protest. He did, however, approve a very limited call-up of reserves following the Tet offensive in 1968.[33] But President Johnson's decision not to employ the National Guard in Vietnam, a decision that many Guardsmen opposed, further emphasized the nation's reliance on active-duty forces to the neglect of its reserve forces in times of conflict. It also made the Guard and reserve havens for those seeking refuge from the draft. Following a highly visible "fact-finding" mission in 1965, Defense Secretary Robert Mc-

Namara and other senior policy-makers had urged President Johnson to call up 235,000 reservists. "We felt that it would be desirable to have a reserve call-up in order to make sure the people of the U.S. knew that we were in a war and not engaged at some two-penny military adventure," said General Earle Wheeler for the Joint Chiefs of Staff.[34]

General William Westmoreland vetoed this proposal on the grounds that the war would last longer than the one-year call-up limitation and recommended that a call-up of reserves be made only when the enemy was near defeat and more American troops could assure it.[35] Johnson followed Westmoreland rather than McNamara on the political grounds of feared reaction by the American people and feared provocation of the Chinese and the Russians. By contrast, President Kennedy's call-up of the reserves in the Berlin crisis in 1961 underscored the importance of the reserve forces both as a political instrument and a deterrent. President Johnson withheld their use, wishing to avoid provocation.[36] During Vietnam, Johnson was intent on preserving a consensus of popular support for his administration and the Vietnam War. The reserves remained unmobilized, and the Vietnam War placed strains on the Regular Army for which it was unprepared and from which it suffered for decades.[37]

Throughout the incessantly turbulent Vietnam years, the McNamara leadership at the Defense Department maintained an effort both to merge and modernize the reserve forces, primarily by attempting to bring the reserves into the National Guard. Ultimately, the effort failed, but it involved shaking up, sifting, and shifting units "at a dizzying pace." There was a substantial reduction in the size of the reserve component and a great deal of experimentation. The cuts and constant changes presented staggering problems to the Guard leadership, which felt itself being used like pawns.[38] This period also brought the Guard out for domestic disturbance-control roles almost as unpleasant and tragic as the labor-unrest missions nearly a century before. In the twenty-two years between 1945 and 1967, state authorities used the National Guard to preserve order seventy-two times, involving almost 200,000 citizen-soldiers in twenty-eight states. Following the assassination of Martin Luther King, Jr., in 1968, 150,000 Guardsmen were called out to intervene in over a hundred disturbances.[39]

The closing years of the divisive Vietnam conflict led to yet another review of regular-reserve relationships. This review produced the Total Force policy, a post-Vietnam recognition that a two-army nation was a confused nation. According to the Total Force concept, both Guard and reserve units were to be properly trained and equipped, integrated into active-duty Regular Army units, and prepared for immediate mobilization and deployment into operational theaters. The round-out concept was adopted whereby designated National Guard brigades were assigned as the third combat component of active Regular Army divisions. One of the principal proponents of this concept was then Army Chief of Staff General Creighton Abrams. Abrams urged that Army National Guard and Reserve combat support and combat service support units replace their counterparts in the Regular Army. This would require immediate mobilization of these units in times of conflict. His argument in this regard was classic. Abrams believed that mobilization of reserve units in Vietnam would have required President Johnson to explain his war aims openly and would have tied local communities to the war effort as well.[40] Implementation of the Total Force concept helped overcome biases by military careerists against "weekend warriors," because it enabled Guardsmen and reservists to work side by side with their active-force colleagues. Where the Total Force concept has been tried, this bias has been largely replaced by the realization by active-duty forces that citizen-soldiers are first-rate military professionals.[41]

The Total Force concept was tried, with conflicting interpretations of its effectiveness, in the Persian Gulf War. Predictably, Regular Army officials claim that National Guard units mobilized for this war did not meet readiness standards and therefore could not be assigned to combat roles. National Guard officials hotly dispute this, arguing that, in keeping with its history, the Regular Army was eager to find deficiencies, that any which did exist were attributable to faults in the Army's training and equipping of the Guard, and finally that the Regular Army had an institutional bias against allowing the National Guard to prove its capability of carrying out its Total Force role. National Guard officials believe to this day that the Army's negative evaluations of Army National Guard brigade readiness were biased—the result of "cooking the books."

The official Department of Defense report on the Persian Gulf War called attention to the substantial, but mostly noncombatant, role played by reserve forces: "Operations Desert Shield and Desert Storm required the largest mobilization and deployment of Reserve Component forces since the Korean Conflict." A more or less neutral observer and an authority on strategy, Colonel Harry G. Summers, Jr., paints an overall positive picture of the role of 230,000 reserve forces ordered to active duty in the Persian Gulf. The comparison with the Korean War is apt, according to Summers, in that the Korean War would have been lost without the reserves. And in the Persian Gulf, without reserve support, active-duty military units simply would have been overwhelmed. He points out that much of the U.S. airlift capability was provided by Air National Guard and Air Reserve units, and a large proportion of the Army's logistics units came from the Reserve Component.[42] Summers notes that 70 percent of the Army's combat support and combat service support units came from the reserves, along with 100 percent of the Navy's combat search-and-rescue squadrons and logistic airlift squadrons, 100 percent of the Marine Corps's civil affairs units, and 59 percent of the Air Force's tactical airlift.

Although the round-out concept, involving insertion of National Guard combat brigades into Regular Army combat divisions, proved controversial at best, a number of reserve combat units were activated and deployed. These included two Army field artillery brigades and an engineering command, four Marine infantry battalions and various other Marine reserve combat units, three tactical fighter squadrons and a variety of other combat units from the Air National Guard and Reserve, and two Naval Reserve minesweepers and other naval units. Additionally, for the first time in history the Coast Guard deployed three reserve units in the combat theater.

Colonel Summers concludes from all this that the Gulf War was concrete evidence of the importance of the Reserve Components. The reserves' psychological contributions were validated even more than its physical ones. Public support for the war was almost guaranteed by activating 798 Army, Navy, Air Force, Marine Corps, and Coast Guard Reserve Component units from over two thousand towns and cities in every state across the country. General Edwin H. Burba, Jr., then commander of U.S. Forces Command, told an audience of reservists, "When you come to war, you bring America with you."[43]

In commenting on the round-out brigade concept as applied to Guard combat brigades—which purportedly failed validation requirements for deployment with Regular Army combat divisions in the Persian Gulf—Summers takes an ambiguous position. According to some, he says, the enormous complexities of the modern battlefield make it impossible to train a maneuver (i.e., infantry and armor) brigade on a part-time basis. But others blame the reserve brigades' delay on their late call-up, equipment shortages, and last-minute changes in readiness standards.[44]

More than one military theorist makes the interesting point that a direct correlation exists between the quality of individual Guard and reserve units and the cohesion and stability of the communities from which they come. The stronger the local community, the stronger the reserve force. This is exactly the synergy upon which the notion of a militia defense is based. It works both ways. Strong nation, strong military; strong military, strong nation.[45]

The so-called Bottom-Up Review carried out in 1993 was designed in part to address the problems with Round-Out.[46] According to this review, the Round-Out notion was to be replaced with a "rounded-up" system whereby all ten Regular Army combat divisions would be composed of three active-duty brigades, to be supplemented in wartime with a National

Guard combat brigade. In the following year, the Army designated twelve National Guard infantry brigades, two armor
brigades, and one armored cavalry regiment as so-called enhanced readiness units. These were to be fully manned,
trained and equipped, and modernized at the same level as the
active unit with which they were affiliated. These brigades
were intended to be maintained at a high level of readiness,
ready to be deployed overseas to reinforce active-duty combat
units within ninety days of mobilization, according to Summers.[47] After establishing these enhanced readiness units, the
army followed up by designating eight National Guard divisions as a "strategic reserve combat force" that would be fully
structured but manned, equipped, and maintained at readiness levels less that 100 percent, with a view toward mobilization in case of protracted conflict. This "tiered" structure of
readiness makes eminent common sense given real-world constraints on air- and sea-lift capabilities—that is, the practical
limits on the capacity to move troops, heavy weapons, and
support and logistics to distant locations by sea and by air—
constraints rarely discussed by those who argue for larger
standing military forces.

Despite the two post–Cold War reviews of the regular-
reserve relationship, there is still a strong sense—heightened
by the acrimonious Persian Gulf experience—that late-
twentieth-century military planners have much to learn about
the integration of reserve with regular forces. Recent studies
reveal that mobilization of reserve forces in the Cold War era
have been characterized by confusion, unpreparedness, delays, and ineffective deployments. Having failed to learn from
previous mistakes, succeeding generations of military plan-

ners, commanders, and policy-makers simply repeat the errors of the past. Despite *policies* to the contrary, reserve units are routinely plundered to fill personnel gaps in regular units, thus destroying unit cohesion and effectiveness and causing delays while these units are reconstituted and retrained. Further, as illustrated by Vietnam, the reserves have more often than not been instruments of political rather than military policy. When reserves are called up to make a political point and then left without a genuine military mission, idleness breeds boredom, which in turn breeds incompetence, a result for which the reserves are unjustly blamed. Similarly, partial call-ups featuring individuals, not units, cause personnel management problems and hard feelings between those called up and those left behind. Finally, and most important, because of the existence of serious rivalries between the regular military establishment and its reserve counterpart, much of the blame for unpreparedness of the reserves must be attributed to neglect by active-duty regular officers responsible for Pentagon planning, programming, and budgeting as these affect the reserve component.[48] National Guard officials believe this failure is less a function of neglect and more a lack of will on the part of the Regular Army hierarchy.[49]

Given this checkered post-World War II history, it is necessary to reenvision how a new and healthier relationship of regulars and reserves might be structured for the twenty-first century.

Chapter 6

A Modest Proposal

The United States has an extraordinary opportunity, created by the end of the Cold War, to structure its military forces to address dramatic new global realities and, at the same time, to restore traditional beliefs and values of our republic. Within a decade, the United States should convert much of its permanent, professional, standing military into a force of citizen-soldiers, an army of the people. Such an undertaking will renew a genuine sense of patriotism in future generations of American citizens, return our national defenses to their more natural and rational pre–Cold War state, and better prepare us for the real security threats of the twenty-first century.

For two and a quarter centuries, a shifting but necessary balance has been maintained between local forces originally designed for domestic purposes and federal forces assigned responsibility for national defense. The blending of the Guard, as the local militia, with the active Army, as the force of the national government, for national defense purposes and their continued separation for domestic order purposes—even as the United States made its transition from minor agrarian power to industrial superpower—represents a rarely recognized triumph of American democracy.[1] Preservation of this balance is vital in carrying out the sweeping military reforms advocated in this essay.

American professional soldiers have often found the citizen-soldier troublesome, according to the military historian Weigley, but throughout the country's history the citizen-soldier has served the professional well, not least by linking him, even in spite of himself, to the nation at large. Weigley deplores the executive branch's reluctance to call up the reserves in the Vietnam War as a nascent reflection of an Uptonian, elitist, antireservist philosophy and hopes that the professional and citizen-soldier partnership can be reestablished. He concludes that the duality of the American military tradition has given the U.S. Army both many of its historic perplexities and its best qualities. At once an expert army and a people's army, it has served as the nation's sword without endangering the nation's democracy. Troublesome as the dual military tradition has sometimes been, the very duality of the American military past is an inheritance to be guarded jealously.[2]

This proposal does not aim to disrupt the sophisticated balance between distinct, historic military forces. Nor is there an intention to propose a new foreign policy for the United States in the twenty-first century, although events will force that outcome sooner rather than later. Our military structures and doctrines are outdated because the policy imperatives they are designed to support are outdated, and our policies are outdated because political realities are changing faster than our policy-makers' ability to adjust to them.

This essay attempts to document the two-army tradition in

American history, to recall the roots of the citizen army in classic republican theory, and to expose the disproportionate role of the standing military in the post–Cold War era. History, tradition, and political principles all support a citizen army and a militia nation. The burden is on those promoting the status quo—the maintenance of a Cold War standing army well into the next century—to show why the United States should *not* return to its historic military tradition.

Our strategists, policy-makers, and political leaders will eventually be required by circumstance—domestic concerns, budgets, intractable international tribal conflicts—to substantially reform our outdated military strategies, structures, and doctrines. This debate should begin while it still can be conducted civilly. And it should focus mainly on the primacy of our reserve forces and citizen-soldiers.

We should undertake military reform while the economy is growing and we are at peace—"fix the roof while the sun is shining"—by replacing much of our permanent standing military with well-trained and well-equipped National Guard and reserve forces, a national militia. The mission of the still-substantial permanent forces remaining should focus on rapid response to immediate threats to American lives or precisely defined security interests worldwide. Such missions will require a high degree of mobility and flexibility, imaginative command, unit cohesion, experience and training, and light-weight, low-maintenance weapons and equipment. The "teeth" (combat) to "tail" (logistical support) ratio of our regular forces should be much lower than at present. The air, sea, and land components of these twenty-first-century permanent forces should look much more like special forces designed for quick, decisive action than like the bottom-heavy Cold War army of today.

Conflicts of the future will be more immediate, local, and dynamic than the massive set-piece, attritional, gunpowder wars of the nineteenth and twentieth centuries. Surprise and cunning will become more important than mass and firepower, at least in the short term; and increasing numbers of conflicts will be local and short-term. Regular forces should represent a quick-response intervention capability. Reserve forces should represent mass and firepower. Great armies cannot move faster (at least for long) than their logistical support in any case. The Army's seventy-plus-ton main battle tank consumes more than two gallons of fuel per mile. Even against inferior forces, as in the Persian Gulf, U.S. commanders will only commit their forces when they have the numbers (mass), firepower (including air and sea), and logistical support required to bring decisive force to bear at the critical point(s). Movement of this modern Cold War military partway around the world, involving massive air and sea lift, takes considerable time. It took over half a year for the United States and its coalition partners to achieve numerical parity and the technological superiority required to dislodge a qualitatively inferior Iraqi army from Kuwait. Though coalition casualties were minimal, financial costs of the operation to the United States substantially exceeded $100 billion (only part of which was recouped from oil-importing allies).

Clearly, such major commitments of massive military forces for sustained operations in the future will require considerable time to plan, organize, and carry out. This is time in which an already trained and equipped reserve force could be mobilized, brought to the final, necessary level of readiness, transported to the theater of conflict, and integrated into or linked with regular units. Such inconvenience as this arrangement might entail will be felt more by presidents and political leaders tasked with rallying public support for the proposed military commitment than by military commanders tasked with carrying it out. There is nothing in American history to suggest that properly prepared citizen-soldiers fight less well in their nation's defense than those who make soldiering a profession. In fact, there is everything to prove otherwise.[3]

Such a military must, of course, be built upon and around a solid professional core. The regular armed services should be perhaps one-third their present size, thus involving 500,000 to 700,000 full-time Army, Navy, Air Force, and Marine Corps personnel. The principle duties of the regular forces should be to (a) train National Guard and Reserve forces and maintain them at the highest possible skill levels; (b) conduct realistic joint regular-reserve combat training exercises as often as necessary to maintain required readiness levels; (c) manage the procurement of modern weapons systems and equip both regular and reserve forces with the most effective weapons possible; (d) maintain modern, state-of-the-art command, control, communications, and intelligence systems; (e) develop strategies, tactics, and doctrines necessary to prepare regular and reserve forces for the battlefield of the future; and (f) most important, carry out forward-deployed, crisis-response missions.

The regular forces should include elite, rapid-deployment, intervention forces that are highly mobile, immediately ready, highly skilled professionals capable of undertaking quick operations necessary to rescue hostages, selectively support local democratic forces (in conjunction with allies and on a time-limited basis), suppress terrorist activities, and protect American diplomats and civilians in danger abroad.[4] These missions must be carefully defined by military and civilian commanders to prevent "mission creep"—the escalation of military responsibilities beyond reasonable military capabilities. Military commanders must not permit these forces to be misused by eager or ambitious politicians, being prepared to resign their commissions in visible protest rather than lead their troops into unjustified danger. This is a crucial issue in the future structuring of the kind of military forces advocated here. The specific purpose and intent of a citizen army is to engage the American people in the policy decision at the point a military operation takes on a permanent or semipermanent character. For if political leaders wish the professional-regular intervention force to expand its short-term mission in scope or time, they would need to deploy units of the National Guard and Reserve according to tiers of readiness. This action would necessarily deploy both citizen-soldiers and their local communities in a public debate regarding the wisdom of the enterprise.

This is an exercise commanders-in-chief and their military advisors welcome only in theory, believing themselves to possess superior knowledge, experience, and wisdom regarding foreign and military policy generally as well as the explicit facts of the conflict at hand. Further, commanders and policymakers often work with highly classified intelligence reports that they are understandably reluctant to divulge. These arguments, especially the latter, can be very persuasive as applied to political crises and military emergencies. They begin to erode as time and the duration of force deployments lengthen.

If U.S. military forces are sent abroad and political leaders decide to expand their numbers and maintain them overseas for some time, under the proposal put forward here, well-trained and equipped reserves would have to be used. This force of National Guard and reserves[5] would be composed of volunteers who have received a period of basic military training followed by regular drills in local units, summer active-duty assignments with regular forces, and upgrade training. Educational grants, training opportunities, basic pay, and other benefits would be provided for National Guard and reserve volunteers. Officers would principally be National Guard officers for the Guard, but in certain cases might include active-duty regulars, retired (but of service age) regulars, and graduates of reserve officer training programs. Sizing the reserve forces would be a function of sober and professional military threat assessments and political definitions of the national security interest sufficiently persuasive to muster broad-based public support. Readiness of the citizen-soldiers would be the responsibility of their officers, under the supervision of the regular forces (as contemplated in Article I, section 8, paragraph 16 of the U. S. Constitution). Readiness standards would vary according to the function and mission each reserve unit was assigned to perform and would be structured according to tiers of need and deployability.

Two key components of a twenty-first-century military structure combining a smaller standing army and a larger national militia, or army of the people, are the concept of *domi-*

nant battlespace knowledge (or more broadly the "revolution in military affairs") and the concept of *tiered readiness*. The first hypothesizes the use of U.S. technological superiority to manage combat operations more intelligently, and the second structures military forces according to when they are needed and can be ready for deployment. Proponents of the revolution in military affairs include former Secretary of Defense William Perry; former chairman of the Joint Chiefs John Shalikashvili; vice-chairman of the Joint Chiefs, Admiral William Owens; and director of net assessments at the Defense Department, Andrew Marshall. Proponents of tiered readiness include an increasing number of knowledgeable public and private critics of the status quo.

The revolution in military affairs (RMA) combines U.S. superiority in intelligence collection, surveillance, and reconnaissance with new systems for command, control, communications, computer systems, and intelligence processing, and then connects these with new generations of precision-guided munitions to obtain battlespace domination.[6] Proponents of this revolution share with others the sense that there is no real defense debate in late-twentieth-century America. They acknowledge that the public debate on defense has been more about politics than strategy. The difference between the Republican Congress and the Clinton administration on defense spending, despite partisan rhetoric, is less than 2 percent. There is little evidence of any vision—let alone competing visions—of where the Defense Department ought to be going. Given radical changes in the post-Soviet security environment, the absence of any deeper debate over the long-range meaning and military demands of our national security is remarkable, if not dumbfounding.[7]

The advocates of RMA believe that a new national consensus on defense should be based upon three premises: first, force structures should be designed that assume technology can substitute for mass and numbers; second, force modernization should use technology to make existing military platforms work better together, operate more efficiently, and employ deadly force at greater distance, speed, and with greater precision; third, superior information technologies should be used to reshape force structures and operational doctrines. Proponents of the revolution in military affairs predict "significant reductions in current [active duty] force levels" and a defense budget reduced to about $210 billion [contrasted with almost $250 billion presently] early in the twenty-first century.

The central strategic theory of the revolution in military affairs is to use a collection of advanced technological systems to enable smaller, quicker combat units to maneuver at high operational tempos in order to destroy an opponent's will and dismantle, rather than annihilate, his military forces. In a word, it is the use of superior advanced technology to perfect maneuver warfare theory. Over a decade, the RMA approach would shift some of the current heavy divisions of the Regular Army and Marines to National Guard and reserve forces and substitute for them "new maneuver groups" or small, highly mobile combat teams. Major naval combatants, including aircraft carriers and attack submarines, would be reduced and be replaced in part by arsenal ships and the new mobile offshore base (MOB) or "movable American island" ships. These are newly configured floating platforms that operate as offshore bases providing supply and resupply of personnel and matériel for intervention forces, particularly in third-world environments where established U. S. resupply is not readily available.

More specifically, the RMA approach envisions reducing Regular Army heavy divisions from six to two, eliminating three separate brigades, reduction of Marine regiments from seven to six, and creating sixteen "new maneuver groups." Manpower levels would experience equivalent reductions: from 495,000 to 300,000 in the Regular Army, and from 174,000 to 126,000 in the Marine Corps. RMA advocates acknowledge problems of transitioning from the current Cold War–type military structure to the lighter, more mobile, technological force of the twenty-first century. Reserve forces, including the National Guard, are a key to the transition. Reserves would assume many of the peacetime commitments now assigned to active forces, according to RMA planners, who note that reservists have increasingly met peacetime operational requirements. The RMA force approach would expand reserve responsibilities considerably."[8]

The RMA plan proposes that the Regular Army and Marine Corps heavy divisions and other reduced units be integrated into the reserve forces. Ground-force reserves would constitute both the base for expansion and the bulk of the traditional ground forces in the event of mobilization. Further, they would become "the center of gravity" of the traditional ground forces, having received most of the equipment and expertise of the heavy units transferred out of the active-duty regular forces. In the first phase of reform, active-duty forces would become the vanguard of the new Army; these forces would be lighter, more agile, more mobile, and more technological. In the second phase, reserve forces would transition into the traditional role of today's Army; these would be heavier, follow-on, echeloned forces.[9]

Acknowledging the military structure's resistance to reform, RMA advocates argue that the RMA force is consciously designed to be more adaptable to change and to ambiguity. It is a military force that rests ultimately not on mass but on brains, not on overwhelming power but on decisive power, not on rigidity but on adaptability, flexibility, and agility. It is a force designed for the age of confusion.

Arguably, the RMA approach places too much confidence in the technological solution. There are reports that early tests of new systems in the RMA mix have overwhelmed both troops and commanders with unassimilated information in quantities too great to be useful. Nevertheless, the very fact that senior military officials, uniformed and civilian, appreciate the potential of advanced technology for historic reform of military structures, organizations, and doctrines is significant for this proposal. So long as it does not become an object of blind worship, America's technological advantage can provide the fulcrum for creating a new and more balanced mix of regular and reserve forces. Such reforms would result in force structures very similar to those advocated here: regular active-duty forces as the point of the spear, and well-trained, well-equipped reserve forces as the spear's shaft.

Although not incorporated explicitly in the "revolution in military affairs" scheme, some concept such as tiered readiness—or varying levels of preparedness according to the timing of the mission—is also implicit in this doctrine. The notion of tiered readiness is one that has begun to receive increased attention in military circles. U.S. Senator John McCain, for one, has proposed a system of three tiers for combat and support forces.[10] According to McCain, the first tier requires forward-deployed and crisis-response forces to be ready for deployment in a matter of days, which is to say virtually immediately. Units such as the 82nd Airborne Division would deploy aboard round-trip–capable aircraft, and Army and Marine brigades afloat could be deployed quickly by existing sea lift. The second tier of readiness involves the follow-on forces required to back up forward-deployed and crisis-response forces. A major buildup in the theater would include initial Army contingency corps divisions, additional Army pre-positioned forces already afloat, naval follow-on forces from the United States, and initial reserve unit activations. The second-tier forces must achieve combat-ready status and be capable of deployment within weeks, not days, after conflict erupts, and must therefore be capable of returning to a high state of readiness "within a short time." The third tier involves conflict resolution forces not required in the theater of operations until after about the sixth month of the conflict's existence, and, therefore, they would have sufficient time to prepare for deployment. Part of the reason these forces have a six-month window is the limitation on air and sea lift capacity and the inability of the theater, in many cases, to absorb major new troop deployments. McCain admits that he would risk some degradation in readiness in the third-tier forces as a mean of redirecting resources toward force (weapons) modernization.

The flaw in the McCain scenario is the minimal support role to which he would commit the Guard and reserves. "Combat arms units in the Guard and Reserves that cannot be mobilized within a very short period of time cannot play a decisive role in conflict resolution," he argues. But he does not explain why Guard and reserve units cannot be ready for deployment within the third (conflict resolution) tier which, due to admitted limits on lift capacity, would not be deployed for six months, much longer than a "very short period of time."

The notion of tiered force readiness is crucial to any return to a predominantly citizen army. But it cannot become a central premise of a twenty-first-century military reform movement without vital incorporation of the National Guard and reserves, at least in conflict resolution (third-tier) combat roles and missions. No good reason is offered in the McCain proposal as to why this cannot be achieved.

At least one analyst, reserve officer Carleton Meyer, has presented a concrete proposal for force reorganization that shifts an increasing combat responsibility to well-trained National Guard and reserve forces while maintaining more than enough military capability to meet U.S. national security commitments. Starting with the ten Army divisions resulting from the 1993 Bottom-Up Review, Meyer proposes forces structured according to four tiers of readiness.[11] The first tier would be composed of eight fully combat-ready divisions, including the 1st Armored Division stationed in Germany, the 3rd Marine Division in Japan and Hawaii, the 82nd Airborne and 101st Air Assault, the 1st Cavalry, 3rd Mechanized Infantry, and 1st and 2nd Marine Divisions. This tier would be ready to go as is. The second tier would be composed of three divisions, including six fully combat-ready brigades, would include 40 percent reserve manning, and would be combat ready within 60 days. Meyer does not specify where this reserve manning would come from, but since the Army Reserve has very little combat capability at present, it is presumed that the reserve components of the second tier would be combat-ready National Guard units. The third tier, including six divisions with 95 percent reserve manning, would be combat ready within 90 days, the earliest date at which strategic lift capacity would be available after deployment of the first tier. The fourth tier would be eight National Guard divisions combat ready within 180 days.

Meyer is working from a solid factual base. A Brookings Institution study of the U.S. Army Guard and Reserve, conducted toward the close of the Cold War, concluded that the Army reserves of the late 1980s bore unprecedented levels of responsibility for the defense of the United States. They were at their peak peacetime strength. They were assigned missions vital to both the war-fighting capability and sustainability of the U.S. Army. And many of their units were expected to deploy quickly as active units. Military operations that the Army could conduct without involving its reserve components appeared at that time to be extremely limited.[12]

In this regard, it is worth noting that 50 percent of regular troops have less than two years of active-duty experience, and more than 50 percent of reserve troops have more than two years' active service.[13] Further, distance learning and new information and communications technologies can make reserve instruction, especially on technical matters, much more immediate, timely, and efficient in maintaining reservists at the same skill level as regulars. Given that many Guard and reserve personnel come from the active-duty forces, a gradual drawdown of the regular forces will help build up the ranks of the reserves.

Meyer's plan represents a total ground force structure of 25 U.S. divisions, all of which would have been available within the time frame required for full deployment in the Persian Gulf war. Meyer notes that the force can be augmented by ten fully combat-ready (first-tier) NATO divisions, which can be used for rapid intervention. Additionally, the National Guard already includes both the eight combat divisions necessary for fourth-tier requirements as well as sufficient independent enhanced readiness brigades necessary to meet second-tier requirements.

Even though the Army has been resisting the 4 percent reduction in manpower, amounting to some 20,000 soldiers, required by the Bottom-Up Review to finance modernization, on the grounds that this token reduction will "hollow out" its forces, Meyer argues that his plan "can save over $16 billion a year by eliminating 195,000 active duty positions and relying on National Guardsmen and reservists to augment follow-on forces."[14] This approximates the 200,000 reduction in regular forces proposed by RMA advocates. Such a plan has the further advantage of addressing the cost-growth/weapons-reduction crisis detailed by Charles Spinney by making more funds available for equipment modernization and, more important, for operations, training, and readiness. Even more critically, however, it offers a concrete basis for shifting America's defenses from a very large permanent peacetime standing army to an army of citizen-soldiers, an army of the people. "Although eliminating 195,000 soldiers from the active force may seem like a deep cut," Meyer notes of his proposal, "this will result in a modest reduction in total active duty personnel in the U. S. military from 1.45 million today to 1.25 million by 2002."

Meyer is not alone among strategic thinkers. Stephen Canby has put much of his lifetime into creative structuring of land forces and is a longtime advocate of applying the Dutch reserve system, designated the RIM, or "pipeline," system, to American military force structures. This system fits well with theories of maneuver warfare and echelon deployment (as practiced by the Israelis, previous German armies, and former Soviet forces).[15] The echelon approach, oversimplified, is based upon regular forces undertaking the initial attack, first light, then heavy, with reserve units providing serial waves of follow-on support.

Canby also points out that these reforms in theory, doctrine, and force structure can help correct Defense Department budget misallocations. Two-thirds of current budgets go to disproportionately large personnel costs required to maintain a larger-than-necessary standing army, while operations and maintenance costs are almost fifteen times greater than those of the Israelis (who often have the same or similar equipment).

Although Meyer's proposals focus specifically on the Army, the same principles apply across all services. Innovative proposals have also been put forward for naval reforms. A rejuvenated merchant fleet can be designed so that modern merchant hulls are equipped to accept modularized weapons and sensor suites that are designed to be replaced as technology advances. In peacetime, these ships can carry out normal civilian maritime functions. In times of conflict, such as in the Persian Gulf War, the same ships can quickly be outfitted with state-of-the-art weapons and sensors to become part of our strategic lift, conveying troops and matériel to military theaters, or can even function as naval combatants. Naval air reserve units can be trained and equipped to work as closely with their active-duty counterparts as the Air National Guard does with the regular Air Force. The Marines have gone so far as to virtually eliminate the distinction between the regular Marine Corps and Marine reserves.

Of all the services, the Air National Guard and Air Force Reserve represent the most successful integration of regulars and reservists. The explanation often given is, "the Air Force has the most interesting toys to play with." Whether or not one accepts this simplistic sociology, the result remains. The Air Force has made the system work: "The Air Reserve forces present a textbook case of success for the total-force policy."[16] Air Reserve squadrons have the highest manning rates and the highest retention percentage of retired regulars in reserve capacities. Their units are almost always able to mobilize and deploy within seventy-two hours, and they routinely meet the operational readiness inspections applied to the regular Air Force. Air National Guard personnel maintain combat aircraft on an around-the-clock, peacetime alert basis and, with the Air Force Reserve, regularly refuel Strategic Air Command bombers. Reservists and Guards regularly train in active Air Force aircraft such as C-141s in peacetime missions, and those reserve crews are indistinguishable from active-force crews.[17]

The success of the regular Air Force–Air National Guard marriage is also attributed to the fact that high school graduates, if they volunteer at all, usually chose the Air Guard because of the glamour of flying. Over 85 percent of the Air Guard recruits were high school graduates, contrasting with 44.4 percent for the Army. Because of this, the Air Force transferred up-to-date planes to the Guard as often as it could, and Air Guard units were routinely provided roles in foreign deployments and engagements.[18]

The current mix in the Air Force is approximately 65 percent active-duty and 35 percent reserve. Some proposals have that mix approaching 50-50 in the foreseeable future, and Charles Spinney believes that up to 80 percent of the total Air Force capability might eventually rest with the Air National Guard and Reserve. Current limitations often have mostly to do with shortages of equipment for Air Guard units, and some Air National Guard bases are grossly underutilized.

General John B. Conaway, former chief of the National Guard Bureau, believes that unit cohesion achieved by maximizing community-based air reserve forces can be as important to the air forces as to the ground forces. Both air crews and ground maintenance personnel perform best when they are stable over time and can develop working knowledge not only of aircraft types but of individual aircraft. The Air Reserve and Guard have even greater personnel stability than the regular Air Force. Overall, the successful regular-reserve relationship in the Air Force can be the best model for all services in a citizen-based twenty-first-century military.

Although this essay has taken pains to avoid basing its arguments on budget considerations, costs are certainly an issue. It is a simple fact that reserve Army units' personnel costs are between four and five times *less* than active-duty units of the same size. Reserve operational activity or tempo rates are also lower than for active-duty forces, thus reducing costs of operations and maintenance of equipment. Obviously, these differences would narrow as reserve forces were brought to higher degrees of training and readiness, but some savings would remain.[19]

Experts seem in general agreement that there can be a Total Force Army in fact if the right steps are taken. Reserves must be seen as an integral part of active-duty units, especially at the combat division level. Whether this concept is called round-up, round-out, or something else matters less than that the reserve unit is given the opportunity to exercise in a realistic combat environment with the same regular unit that it would augment in an actual conflict scenario. During the early 1960s, and especially with the call-up of reservists during the Berlin crisis, the American military pursued a policy of mobilizing reservists to fill individual slots rather than deploying them in units.[20] This fragmentary mobilization sustains the traditional National Guardsman's theory that, regardless of statute, *there is no such thing as an Army ready reservist who is not a participating member of a unit undergoing regularly scheduled and periodic training.*[21]

Both combat and combat-support reserve units must be provided modern equipment that is not procured at the expense of regular units or at the sufferance of the Regular Army. The importance of this factor cannot be overstated. Even as deployment is constrained by air and sea lift capacity, so is reserve effectiveness almost totally dependent on the quality and quantity of the equipment available in both the training and operating phases. Industrial lead times required to retool for military procurement are substantial. Thus, most wars are "come as you are," that is, "bring what you've got." The possibility of "short-notice war" is ever present. But short-notice acceleration of industrial output for defense production is not.[22]

Training must be more effective (e.g., force-on-force "free play" training) and based more on realistic readiness expectations. Either reserve units should not be expected to meet readiness and deployability standards beyond the funds available to them, *or* sufficient funds should be made available to enable these units to maintain realistic deployability standards. Threat assessments should be made more realistic and deployment times and readiness levels should be realistically linked to those assessments. Threat assessments that are unrealistically high or wide will never be met by reserve forces.[23]

Much of the traditional regular-reserve tension will be alleviated as active-duty regulars train and operate with their reserve counterparts with sufficient regularity that the reserves are accepted as military professionals in every respect. Recognition of reservists' professionalism reinforces military élan and contributes to a higher state of combat readiness, and active-duty forces develop greater understanding and respect for reserve forces.[24] The more frequently reserves participate in mobilization exercises, the more realistic their field training, and the more they are tested according to active-duty performance standards, the closer the regular-reserve integration will be. Peacetime preassignment of Guard and reserve units to the active-force units with which they will fight in wartime is a vital component of this integration.[25] The pattern already established between Air Force active-duty and reserve forces, as we have seen, proves the value of this approach, whose key is making the commanders of the active-duty units responsible for the combat readiness of their augmented Guard and reserve units.

Sufficient incentives, in the form of pay and benefits, technical training, education grants, experience with advanced technologies, and the challenge of combat assignments are available to meet the manpower needs of regular active-duty forces as well as the enhanced requirements of a fully integrated National Guard and reserve. These incentives are even more potent when reinforced by national values that elevate and reward civic duty, national service, and the militia principle.

In sum, there are several keys to creating effective U.S. reserve forces in the twenty-first century. First, training of the reserve forces should be real, continuous, and strenuous. Serious demands of time and attention should be attached to reserve service for a citizen army to be effective. Second, reservists should be trained with state-of-the-art, not second-hand, equipment. The Air National Guard is the best proof of the close tie between effectiveness and top-of-the-line equipment. Access to the nation's best technology is a powerful inducement for the sacrifice involved in a reserve commitment. But it can also produce better soldiers and more productive citizens. Third, reservists must be fully integrated into and train with regular combat units. This integration more than anything else will establish the standard that reservists must be ready to go on the shortest notice. Fourth, there must be adequate air and sea lift for reserve combat and combat-support units to get to the theater of conflict. Finally, given their complex dual-status history, National Guard units must be clear on the authority of the federal government to nationalize and order them into combat. This point may seem obvious, but the issue was raised as recently as the Panama invasion in the early 1990s when several state governors attempted to block federal mobilization of Guard units on political grounds.[26]

Endless changes can be rung on this proposal. The devil, in this case, is not in the details. At issue is whether the United States will continue a Cold War military indefinitely into the twenty-first century, well after its mission has ended, spending itself into numerical weakness in weaponry and searching for new demons to justify its existence. The fundamental issue is not one of force structures but of common sense and practical political philosophy. Should a democratic republic perpetuate a large permanent standing army when its security is not threatened and when, collectively with its allies, it possesses more than enough power to isolate and suppress local conflicts? The National Guard will help keep alive the citizen-soldier tradition and the division of military power within our federal system. Its existence is important in preventing the United States from ever becoming a militaristic power. Throughout the Cold War era, the nation has been military, but never, now or before, militaristic. For a democratic republic, there is a life-and-death difference.[27]

Depending on world conditions, pursuing a plan like the RMA, or McCain's, or Meyer's for the next five years leaves open the possibility of further "right-sizing" in the years beyond. If, as many have speculated, we are entering a century of globalized trade and finance, absent the ideological extremism and nation-state world wars that characterized the twentieth century, it is not unreasonable to envision a U.S. military force structure that is formed on the concept of tiered readiness and is composed of a professional core of a half-million active duty, permanent military personnel supported by a million or more highly trained, fully equipped citizen reservists. Under this approach, the roles of the active-duty regulars would include strategic planning and preparation of doctrine and tactics; maintenance of the technology base and weapons design and procurement systems; guaranteeing the integrity of command, control, communications, intelligence, and military education systems; training, equipping, and preparing the army of citizen reservists.

The reserve ranks would be filled by actively recruiting the ablest volunteers. Reasonable pay scales would be maintained for all reservists, with special education, training, and pay incentives for those possessing special skills. Employers might receive tax incentives for conducting joint job-training programs with the military and encouraging employees to join reserve units. Although generous education benefits could be made available to all reservists, possibly through a voucher system, benefits would increase for those volunteering for high-readiness units requiring extraordinary time commitments. Access to new and high-technology equipment and weaponry would be a special inducement for many volunteers.

Individual reserve units up to and beyond brigade levels would be regularly and scrupulously tested by active-duty cadres that would be held responsible by senior military and civilian commanders as well as by Congress for maintaining prescribed degrees of readiness. Unlike the Gulf War experience, following which finger-pointing still continues over readiness of National Guard brigades, validation of readiness requirements for all reserve units would be required by both routine training exercises and by "fire-drill" call-ups.

Absent a serious national security threat or national peril, there is currently little support for a system of universal national service or even universal military training. But the notion of common responsibility for the common defense has rich roots in classic republican theory and practice. At the very least, our nation should maintain a voluntary national service opportunity, encompassing military and civilian options, both with educational benefits, for all young people who wish to serve their country. But our leadership should also go beyond this by courageously advocating a system of universal military training.

The republican ideal is dependent upon civic virtue, the engagement of the citizen in the life of the society and nation. Nothing is as central to a republic as its defense and security. Nothing would more likely reawaken a dormant sense of patriotism in American young people than a universal national training requirement. Nothing would engage the American people in the conduct of their international relations more profoundly than having their sons and daughters more directly involved in the national defense. For those young people wishing to convert their training into service, whether in active duty or reserve forces, generous education benefits would provide sufficient incentive and reward and would more than repay taxpayers in the increased lifelong productivity of the beneficiaries.

The central objective of a citizen defense is to engage the public in decisions regarding deployment of expeditionary forces to take part in overseas military ventures. The public will be involved in those decisions to the degree the reserve forces are integrated into the active-duty regular forces. Therefore, something like the Total Force philosophy is crucial for any democracy. Since reserve forces are community based, citizens and communities will also become more involved in defense budget issues—how money is spent, why reserve equipment isn't more modern, why expensive equipment does not work. What some would like to remain within the esoteric environment of Washington will be brought closer to Main Street. This is what is meant by an army of the people.

Otherwise, political and military leaders will be powerfully tempted to play Great Power games, using standing armies as chess pieces in the never-ending struggle for hegemony, influence, and prestige. Being a powerful nation, the United States must accept leadership responsibilities. But these must be clearly defined and must in all cases require the engagement of the American people. The next century offers the opportunity for the United States to maintain a high degree of security, contribute substantially to international peacekeeping missions, and still not depend upon a disproportionately large standing army.

The twenty-first-century threats to America's security and continuity are not primarily military and therefore cannot be defeated by professional armies. They are cultural and will be answered, if at all, by national unity, which itself will be strengthened by citizen-soldiers and restoration of an army of the people.

Notes

Chapter 1. A Conspiracy of Silence: Why Doesn't Anyone Question the Military Status Quo?

1. See generally, Martin van Creveld, *The Transformation of War* (Free Press, 1991).
2. Barbara Tuchman, *The March of Folly* (Knopf, 1984), pp. 4–33.
3. This is not to say the twenty-first century is without dangers. Iran, Iraq, North Korea, and others possess the potential to create regional conflict that may or may not directly affect U.S. interests. There are also "rogue" nations such as Libya. Some still fear a resurgent Russia and others foresee an aggressive China. The greatest threats to world peace come from post–Cold War disintegration, however, and they are analyzed at length in this essay. By and large, they do not lend themselves to resolution by the force structures created to contain the Soviet threat.
4. The present process is based upon the premise that the will of the people will be expressed on these vital issues by their representatives in Congress. Given the real erosion in public confidence in political authority, this process might or might not operate satisfactorily in future conflicts involving "interests" and murky values.
5. The term "careerists" refers to what are usually called military "professionals." Throughout this essay, the word "professional" is used to describe the permanent standing military. In this connection, it is used to denote those for whom military service is a paid occupation, not necessarily those possessing superior competence or skill. Indeed, one of my arguments is that, properly trained and equipped, citizen-soldiers—classic militia, National Guard, and reserves—are as professional as those who make military service a career.
6. Carl von Clausewitz, *On War* (Princeton University Press, 1976).
7. Professor I. B. Holley, Jr., properly questions this summary formulation as suggesting isolationism. Nothing less characterizes the author's public and private careers. For more than twenty-five years, I have vigorously advocated greater U.S. economic, political, and diplomatic participation in the global community.

8. It is certainly legitimate to argue that the Persian Gulf War was waged to punish Iraqi aggression against Kuwait. However, other acts of cross-border aggression in areas of the world where international oil supplies have not been at stake have failed to draw the equivalent military attention by the United States and other oil-importing nations.

9. Allen Millet and Peter Maslowski, *For the Common Defense: A Military History of the United States of America* (Free Press, 1984), p. 408. A total of 16.3 million Americans wore uniforms between 1941 and 1946, of whom more than 10 million were processed through the Selective Service System.

10. I was surprised, and a bit shocked, at the degree to which retired military officers who reviewed this manuscript expressed genuine skepticism about the ability of average Americans to understand and judge foreign policy and military matters.

11. These principles are taken from "Enlightened Engagement: A Foreign Policy Framework for the 21st Century," lectures delivered by the author, Georgetown University, June 11–13, 1986. Very similar principles were stated by Secretary of Defense Caspar Weinberger at the National Press Club, November 28, 1984.

12. I am acutely aware of the multiple complexities surrounding this proposal. Financially, it will be expensive in implementation. Politically, it will be resisted by many on the left as militaristic and by many on the right as statist. Socially, it will be resisted by many young people as undue interference in their lives, especially in peacetime. Practically, it can only be implemented over time and after considerable study and preparation. A system of universal national training is justifiable *only* if it can be made compatible with the greater long-term goal of reduction of the permanent standing force. It is advocated principally to remain faithful to the classic republican theory and practice, premised on civic duty, upon which this essay is founded.

13. John Keegan, *The History of Warfare* (Knopf, 1993), p. 232.

Chapter 2. The Transformation of War

1. Robert Kaplan, *The Ends of the Earth: A Journey at the Dawn of the 21st Century* (Vintage Books, 1996), p. 8.

2. Kaplan, Robert, "The Coming Anarchy," *Atlantic Monthly* (February, 1994).

3. Kaplan, *The Ends of the Earth*, p. 21.

4. Martin van Creveld, *The Transformation of War* (Free Press, 1991).

5. *Ibid.*, pp. ix, 224.

6. *Ibid.*, p. 36.

7. *Ibid.*, p. 160, 61.

8. *Ibid.*, p. 204.

9. *Ibid.,* p. 225.
10. Samuel P. Huntington, *The Clash of Civilizations and the Remaking of World Order* (Simon & Schuster, 1996).
11. *Ibid.,* p. 28.
12. *Ibid.,* p. 20.
13. *Ibid.,* p. 246.
14. *Ibid.,* p. 247.
15. *Ibid.,* p. 272.
16. van Creveld, *op. cit.,* p. 107 (Emphasis added).
17. Carleton Meyer, "Rightsizing Our 21 Division Army" and "Demobilizing the Army," unpublished papers, September 20, 1996.
18. *Ibid.*
20. *Ibid.,* p. 212 (Emphasis added).
21. Kaplan, *The Ends of the Earth,* p. 9.
22. Interview with Hazel O'Leary, *New York Times,* January 25, 1997 (Emphasis added).
23. *Ibid.,* (Emphasis added).

Chapter 3. The Mysterious Disappearance of the "Peace Dividend"

1. William Greider, "Fortress America," *Rolling Stone,* p. 61, July 10–14, 1997.
2. *Ibid.*
3. *Ibid.,* p. 62.
4. According to one retired senior military officer: "Army leaders (division commanders) responsible for readiness/capability of their Guard r/o [round-out] brigades were promoted. In the Air Force, they would have been fired."
5. Franklin C. Spinney, "Defense Spending Time Bomb?," *Challenge: The Magazine of Economic Affairs,* pp. 7–8, July–August, 1996.
6. *Ibid.*
7. Franklin C. Spinney, "Defense Power Games," unpublished paper.
8. *Ibid.*
9. *Ibid.*
10. Franklin C. Spinney, "Anatomy of Decline," unpublished paper, July 29, 1996.
11. *Ibid.* One senior retired officer said, "I agree in spades." Another said, "Yes!"
12. Stress is placed on the conditional *could* because no clear proof is available for this assertion. It is offered as a testament to the common sense of the ordinary American.
13. Interview with William Lind, September 15, 1996. At least one retired officer agrees: "Military officers have often said—'when working in the Pentagon no one judges your military skills or qualities; you are judged by how much dollars you bring to your agency.'"

Chapter 4. The Republic and the Militia

1. Jerry Cooper, *The Militia and the National Guard in America Since Colonial Times: A Research Guide* (Greenwood Press, 1993), p. 16.
2. E. Wayne Carp, "Early American Military History: a Review of Recent Work," *Virginia Magazine of History and Biography* 94 (July 1986), p. 276.
3. Cooper, *op. cit.,* p. 15
4. *Ibid.,* p. 44.
5. Victor Davis Hanson, *The Western Way of War* (Knopf, 1989), pp. 4, 5.
6. Michael M. Sage, *Warfare in Ancient Greece* (Routledge, 1996), p. 35.
7. John Rich and Graham Shipley, *War and Society in the Greek World* (Routledge, 1993), pp. 20, 87.
8. Sage, *op. cit.,* p. 34.
9. Thucydides, *The Peloponnesian War,* in Robert Strassler, ed., *The Landmark Thucydides* (Free Press, 1996), bks. 6 and 7.
10. *Ibid.,* pp. 524, 258.
11. Sage, *op. cit.,* p. 35.
12. *Ibid.,* p. 150.
13. *Roman Antiquities,* X.17, E. Cary, trans., quoted in Michael Grant, ed., *Readings in the Classical Historians* (Scribners, 1992), pp. 353–4. See also, Niccolò Machiavelli, *Discourses on Livy,* Harvey Mansfield and Nathan Tarcow, trans. (University of Chicago, 1996), pp. 271–2.
14. John Rich and Graham Shipley, *War and Society in the Roman World* (Routledge, 1993), p. 95. 96.
15. *Ibid.,* p. 7 (Emphasis added).
16. J. G. A. Pocock, *The Machiavellian Moment: Florentine Political Thought and the Atlantic Republican Tradition* (Princeton University Press, 1975), pp. 202, 203.
17. *Ibid.,* p. 406, 412.
18. Leopold Von Ranke, *A History of England* (Oxford, 1875), p. 483.
19. Pocock, *op. cit.,* p. 386.
20. *Ibid.,* p. 410.
21. Millet and Maslowski, *op. cit.,* pp. 2, 3.
22. *Ibid.,* p. 4, 5.
23. *Ibid.,* p. 62.
24. Pocock, *op. cit.,* p. 528.
25. William Blackstone, *Commentaries on the Laws of England* (1783).
26. Millet and Maslowski, *op. cit.,* p. 85.
27. *Ibid.,* p. 86.
28. It is an interesting, and not irrelevant, question whether engagement in international commerce necessarily entails maintenance of an international military

presence to protect and promote those commercial interests. It would be a fascinating study to analyze the historic connection between the two. Based upon history's evidence, will the twenty-first-century global economy be one in which disputes can be resolved in international arenas of mediation, such as the World Trade Organization and GATT, or will participants and competitors all be required to maintain fleets and bases abroad to protect their commercial interests? To my knowledge, no one has properly addressed this issue.

29. Clinton Rossiter, ed., *The Federalist Papers,* no. 24 (Mentor, 1961).

30. *Ibid.,* no. 26.

31. *Ibid.,* no. 25.

32. *Ibid.,* no. 29.

33. John K. Mahon, *History of the Militia and the National Guard* (Macmillan, 1983), p. 3.

34. Bernard Bialyn, *The Ideological Origins of the American Revolution* (Harvard University Press, 1967), p. 338.

35. Ralph Ketcham, ed., *The Anti-Federalist Papers and The Constitutional Convention Debates* (Mentor, 1986), Patrick Henry, May 6, 1788.

36. *Ibid.,* "Brutus," no. X, January 24, 1788.

37. Bailyn, *op. cit.,* p. 340.

38. Henry, *The Anti-Federalist Papers, op. cit.*

39. Bailyn, *op. cit.,* p. 340.

40. Ketcham, *op. cit.,* introduction.

41. Julian Boyd, ed., *The Papers of Thomas Jefferson* (Princeton University Press, 1950).

42. Russell F. Weigley, *History of the United States Army* (Macmillan, 1967), p. 104.

43. Pocock, *op. cit.,* pp. 528, 29.

44. Ketcham, *op. cit.,* p. 221.

45. Rossiter, *op. cit.,* no. 46.

46. Keegan, *op. cit.,* p. 353.

47. Cooper, *op. cit.,* p. 16.

48. Alexis deTocqueville, *Democracy in America* (Knopf, 1985), no. 49.

49. *Ibid.,* no. 23.

50. *Ibid.,* no. 22.

51. *Ibid.,* no. 49.

52. *Ibid.,* no. 22.

Chapter 5. Why Do We Have Two Armies?

1. Emory Upton, *The Military Policy of the United States* (Greenwood Press, 1968).

2. Weigley, *op. cit.,* p. xi.

3. Mahon, *op. cit.,* p. 29.

4. *Cooper,* op. cit., p. 22.

5. Millet and Maslowski, *op. cit.,* p. 262.

6. *Ibid.,* p. 249.

7. Mahon, *op. cit.,* p. 125.

8. Millet and Maslowski, *op. cit.,* p. 273.

9. I. B. Holley, Jr., *General John M. Palmer, Citizen Soldiers and the Army of a Democracy* (Greenwood Press, 1982), p. 95.

10. *Ibid.,* p. 391.

11. *Ibid.,* pp. 555, 56.

12. John M. Palmer, *Statesmanship or War* (Doubleday, Doran Co., 1927).

13. Holley, *op. cit.,* p. 714.

14. *Ibid.,* p. 714.

15. *Ibid.*

16. Palmer, *op. cit.,* pp. 15, 54.

17. *Ibid.,* p. 27.

18. On this point, Major General Francis S. Greenlief, Ret., writes: "*Army Times* (3 March 1997) reported on an alternative defense strategy. Major General Richard A. Alexander, President of the NGAUS, called this alternative the 'rebuttable presumption' because it presumes that all units would be organized and maintained in the Guard or Reserve unless an adequate rebuttal could justify organizing and maintaining specific units in the active duty forces."

19. Palmer, *op. cit.,* p. 128.

20. *Ibid.,* p. 148.

21. *Ibid.,* p. 75.

22. *Ibid.,* p. 74 (Emphasis added).

23. Reprinted in Holley, *op. cit.,* pp. 659, 60.

24. Bennie J. Wilson, III, ed., *The Guard and the Reserve in the Total Force: the First Decade* (National Defense University Press, 1985), p. 39.

25. Cooper, op. cit., p. 124.

26. Millet and Maslowski, *op. cit.,* pp. 313, 14.

27. *Ibid.,* pp. 324, 25.

28. Mahon, *op. cit.,* p. 221.

29. Millet and Maslowski, *op. cit.,* p. 366.

30. *Ibid.,* pp. 366, 67.

31. Quoted in Mahon, *op. cit.,* p. 305.

32. Cooper, *op. cit.,* p. 123.

33. Martin Binkin and William W. Kaufmann, *U.S. Army Guard and Reserve: Rhetoric, Realities, Risks* (The Brookings Institution, 1989), p. 92.

34. Quoted in Larry Berman, *Planning a Tragedy: The Americanization of the War in Vietnam* (Norton, 1982), p. 126.
35. William Westmoreland, *A Soldier Reports* (Doubleday, 1976), pp. 172, 73.
36. Binkin and Kaufmann, *op. cit.,* p. 49.
37. Weigley, *op. cit.,* p. 534.
38. Mahon, *op. cit.,* p. 236.
39. *Ibid.,* p. 241.
40. Cooper, *op. cit.,* p. 129.
41. Wilson, *op. cit.,* p. 45.
42. Harry G. Summers, Jr., *The New World Strategy* (Simon & Schuster, 1995), p. 130.
43. *Ibid.,* p. 133.
44. *Ibid.,* p. 150.
45. Interview with William Lind, September, 1996.
46. The very characterization of the review as "Bottom-Up" was a misnomer, according to one retired general officer who said, "The bottom never was very far from the top."
47. Summers, *op. cit.,* p. 151. The history of these "enhanced readiness" units is confused. One retired senior officer has said, "Of the several retired four-star generals I have worked with, not one ever thought these units would fight as units."
48. Binkin and Kaufmann, *op. cit.,* pp. 61–62.
49. "The unwillingness of the Army to mobilize 'ARNG round-out brigades' for deployment for combat in Desert Storm [the Persian Gulf War], notwithstanding the fact that the ARNG brigades met the standards required of them by the Army and the fact that active Army combat units trained for five months in the desert before they were considered ready for the Army, demonstrates that the Army was trying to justify the position it took in developing the 'Base Force Policy.'" Letter from Major General Francis S. Greenlief, Ret., March 13, 1997.

Chapter 6. A Modest Proposal

1. Wilson, *op. cit.,* p. 25.
2. Weigley, *op. cit.,* p. 556.
3. Wilson, *op. cit.,* pp. 24, 25.
4. This latter mission is well recognized under international law.
5. Even though the Guard finds the idea anathema, some might want to consider a synthesis of the two.
6. James Blaker, "Understanding the Revolution in Military Affairs: A Guide to America's 21st Century Defense," Progressive Policy Institute, Defense Working Paper no. 3, January 1997.

NOTES

7. *Ibid.*

8. *Ibid.*

9. *Ibid.*

10. John S. McCain, III, "Ready Tomorrow: Defending American Interests in the 21st Century," unpublished paper, March 1996.

11. Carleton Meyer, "Rightsizing Our 21 Division Army" and "Demobilizing the Army," unpublished papers, September 20, 1996.

12. Binkin and Kaufmann, *op. cit.,* pp. 18–19.

13. Interview with Major General Edward J. Philbin, Ret., executive director, National Guard Association of the United States, September 1996.

14. Meyer, *op. cit.,* p. 1

15. This is not to say it would necessarily work also with U.S. defense needs. Israeli citizen-soldiers keep their weapons handy and can be deployed to national borders almost immediately. Neither the Germans nor the Soviets represented "armies of the people." Additionally, "The RIM concept allows the active duty forces to retain all the flags and resulting grade structure limiting the 'reservists' to the dogface fighting role." Major General Greenlief.

16. Wilson, *op. cit.,* p. 139.

17. *Ibid.,* p. 117.

18. Mahon, *op. cit.,* p. 254.

19. Binkin and Kaufmann, *op. cit.,* pp. 30, 31.

20. According to retired Major General Greenlief, this statement is only partially true. "USAR personnel not assigned to units (filler personnel) were mobilized as individuals and assigned to units after mobilization (some to ARNG units) according to plan. ARNG units were mobilized, e.g., the 49th Armor Division, TXARNG, and 32nd Infantry Division, WIARNG. Of interest, the 32nd Division was shipped to Ft. Lewis, WA., for post mobilization training. The Army refused to issue winter clothing and equipment already in Army warehouses in Ft. Lewis. The Army responded by calling the 32nd the 'Cry Babies.'"

21. Mahon, *op. cit.,* pp. 148, 149.

22. Wilson, *op. cit.,* p. 150.

23. Binkin and Kaufmann, *op. cit.,* pp. 138, 39.

24. Wilson, *op. cit.,* p. 49,

25. *Ibid.*

26. The issue has to do with whether the president is willing to declare a national emergency or state of war under which conditions mobilization authority over the Guard and Reserve is clear. Confusion arises when the president wants to call up the Guard and Reserve without the required statutory declaration.

27. Mahon, *op. cit.,* p. 267.

Index

size of, 56
size reduction in, 151, 156
tiered readiness and, 158
Marine Corps Reserve, U. S., 56, 143, 163
Mark Antony, 86
Marshall, Andrew, 154
Marshall, George, 123, 127, 132–33
Martin, Luther, 105
Mason, George, 105
Mauldin, Bill, 52
McCain, John, xviii, 158–59, 168
McGovern, George, xviii
McKinley, William, 123
McNamara, Robert, 138–39
Medellin cartel, 31
Mercenary soldiers, 9
  in Greek military, 83–84
  Machiavelli on, 89, 90–91
  in Roman military, 86
Meyer, Carleton, 159–60, 161–62, 168
Middle East, xvi, 6, 50–52
Military Construction Subcommittee, xiv
Military-industrial complex, 3, 7, 133
Military Policy of the United States, The (Upton), 118
Military Reform Caucus, xiv–xv
Militia Act, 120, 135–36
Militias, 21–24, 77–115
  English, 78, 79, 91–95, 104
  Greek, 21–22, 79–84, 90
  private, 23–24
  in Revolutionary War, 77, 78, 95–97, 102
  Roman, 77, 84–87, 90, 103–4
  state versus national, 110
Minutemen, 22, 77, 97, 99
Mission creep, 151
Mobile offshore base (MOB) ships, 155–56
Mogadishu, 2

Nasson, Samuel, 105
National Defense Act of 1916, 120, 136

National Defense Act of 1920, 120, 126, 127–28, 133, 136–37
National Defense Panel (NDP), 58–59
National Guard, U. S., 22, 23, 105, 117–45, 147, 149, 167–68, see also Two-army system
  Air, 56, 142, 163–64, 167
  Army, 55, 160
  benefits suggested for, 153
  for controlling civil unrest, 16, 122, 140
  failure to mobilize in Vietnam War, 14, 138–39
  federal control of, 120–21, 168
  increased role in national military matters, 135–36
  origination of term, 119
  peacetime preassignment in, 166
  readiness of, 133–34, 169–70
  regular military hostility toward, 133–35, 137
  revolution in military affairs and, 155, 156
  round-out brigades of, 59, 60–61, 142, 143
  tiered readiness and, 152, 159, 160
  Total Force concept and, 60–62, 140–41
  training of, 151, 167
National Guard Association, 119, 135
National Guard Bureau, 136, 164
National interest, 39–40
National Security Council, 40
Nation-state wars, 1, 28, 29, 30, 31, 32, 38–39, 40, 46, 50
Native Americans (Indians), 106–7, 114
NATO, 19, 42, 44, 161
Naval Peace Establishment Act, 111
Naval Reserve, U. S., 55, 142, 143
Navy, U. S.
  Adams and, 111–12
  budget of, 41, 62
  mobile offshore base ships and, 155–56
  Persian Gulf War and, 142, 163
  proposed reforms for, 162–63